The Ovens of Brittany

C.O.O.K.B.O.O.K

by
Terese Allen

First edition.
Second printing (revised), 1992

Library of Congress Catalog Number: 91-72656

ISBN: 0-942495-11-X

For additional copies of this book, contact:

Amherst Press
A division of Palmer Publications, Inc.
P.O. Box 296
Amherst, Wisconsin 54406

To JB, my favorite person.

Acknowledgments

The creation of this book has been a real adventure for me. It's a joy to acknowledge the people who, in many small and large ways, were along for this exciting, enlightening ride I've been on. First, and from the bottom of my heart, I thank my generous friend and wise lawyer Bob Kay, who gave his time, shared his knowledge and showed so much patience.

I'm also grateful to Chuck and Roberta Spanbauer, my publishers at Amherst Press, who thrilled me by showing immediate and enthusiastic interest in the book and with whom I've enjoyed working and becoming friends.

Three women must be mentioned who were wonderfully encouraging to me when the book was in its earliest and most uncertain stages. Ann Phillips-Robak's expressions of unswerving confidence in me were like a tonic. Author Margaret Guthrie put a professional stamp of approval on my ideas, gave helpful tips and became a "food-friend." And whenever I needed to talk about it, my friend Barb Kay was one who really listened. A lot.

One of the most pleasurable aspects of writing this cookbook was the recipe-testing, for it gave me endless hours doing what I love—cooking and writing—and it prompted the scheduling of plenty of company to consume and assess the dishes. Thanks go to the many people who "ate it all up" and gave their honest critiques. After I had finished my rounds, the recipes were tested one final time by big-hearted friends, neighbors and family members. I'm grateful for all their help and though space doesn't allow my naming each one, my sister Lutie, who worked on dozens of recipes, deserves special mention and a round of applause.

Another person I'd like to thank is Jim Block, with whom I share my life, and who deserves a whole page of acknowledgment himself. He listened, cared, helped, talked, forgave, encouraged, supported. He also gave backrubs.

Lastly, there's a deepfelt gratitude and respect for all the creative, committed people of the Ovens, past and present. I'd like to take note of the State Street "originals," the people who started it all, and to acknowledge owners Mark and Karen McKean. Thanks go to the cooks and bakers who contributed recipes. To the many Ovens people who answered my millions of questions and helped in so many ways, especially the pastry bakers and other staff at Ovens East. To all my zany and talented co-workers from over the years. And thanks to all the employees and customers of the Ovens community. I'd say I don't know how to fully express my appreciation, except that this cookbook itself, this recording of how it was, is my way of saluting the people of the Ovens of Brittany.

Contents

Introduction vi

Terms and Techniques xii

Appetizers and Soups 1

Salads and Salad Dressings 19

Chicken and Beef 33

Fish and Shellfish 53

Sandwiches, Side Dishes and Vegetarian Choices 63

Breakfast and Brunch Choices 77

Cookies, Muffins and Bakery Choices 91

Pastries 103

Index 123

Introduction

The original Ovens of Brittany opened its doors to the public in Madison, Wisconsin in 1972. My first visit to that unique restaurant located down the street from the State Capitol was a couple of years later. To this day, I can easily conjure up the unexpected enchantments of that occasion: the white-capped, flour-dusted bakers rolling out croissant dough; a spiral staircase leading to the second floor where the old-fashioned ovens could be viewed from above; the deep, irresistible aroma of coffee, fresh-roasted, *fine* coffee; tiny ceramic pots of strawberry jam and sweet butter arranged on marble-topped tables; and my first taste of a dish called a Guthrie Bun—freshly baked brioche, puffed high, stuffed with impossibly delicious beef and mushrooms, with burgundy sauce. I think I was a bit stunned. I simply had had no idea food could be this good or restaurants this delightful. Immediately hooked, I became a regular customer, and in 1982, after a stint at an East coast cooking school, I returned to Madison to launch a restaurant career with the Ovens of Brittany.

Both as a customer and an employee, I hardly could have made a better choice of restaurant, for from its beginning the "Ovens," as the organization is affectionately known, was something truly exceptional. Emphasizing quality ingredients, from-scratch preparation, beautiful atmosphere and gracious service, the Ovens enjoyed immediate popularity with Madison's residents and developed an excellent reputation throughout the Midwest. The love affair that's been going on for nearly twenty years between Madison and the Ovens started with a nine-table gourmet restaurant inspired by the social consciousness of the 1960's; the "fruits" of that love now include six restaurants, five bakeries, a cafeteria outlet, and a large-scale catering operation. And counting.

The Ovens of Brittany Story

The story of the Ovens of Brittany is an evolutionary tale. It all began in the mythical days of the hippie movement when Madison's State Street was most noted for its trashy sidewalks and broken glass, the expression of students frustrated with the Vietnam War. Madison's restaurant scene in 1971, limited to steak houses and pizza parlors, looked nearly as dismal as the boarded windows on State Street.

Living in a large house in Madison at the time was a coterie of idealistic young people who called themselves the Phoenix Academy of Cultural Exploration and Design. Founded by a worldly, charismatic interior designer from Chicago named Jo Annae Guthrie, the group's goal was to develop and effect positive cultural change. In an early statement of purpose, Phoenix members expressed the belief that "positive cultural models can be created which will enrich our present way of life by expressing new patterns of inspiration, beauty, and clarity." The group felt that the creation of cultural models and the "training of the individual in the development of his understanding and strength will promote the inner evolution of Humanity. The marriage of this inner and outer work may lead man closer to Wisdom, and help the world approach the ideal of harmony toward which it strives."

Opening a gourmet restaurant was part of a plan to put their philosophical principles into action as well as support themselves. Under Mrs. Guthrie's leadership, Phoenix members transformed a basement beauty parlor into a replica of a charming, centuries-old restaurant from far-off Brittany, France. The first menu was classical French and highlighted natural ingredients and exquisite dishes prepared to order. The foods, the wines, the music, the decorations, even the way the staff was dressed were all expressions of the Phoenix vision of a cultured, ordered life.

The original group saw themselves as a family and viewed customers as guests. They felt that transforming something as basic as eating and as mundane as business into a beautiful, nurturing experience was a natural way to make life more meaningful, more whole. What they sought was balance, what one longtime employee called "locating the sacred within the profane." Mrs. Guthrie's plan was not necessarily to change the world, but to create a smaller world of beauty and integrity, one that could perform as a model for those involved in it and for those who came into it, even briefly.

Besides the holistic approach, the most unusual thing about the restaurant they called the Ovens of Brittany was that not a single staff member was a food service professional. Richard Borovsky, maitre d'hotel of the first Ovens, remembers when he realized just a few hours before their opening lunch in March of 1972 that no one knew on which side of the plates the forks were supposed to be placed. Luckily, a friend who was attending culinary school at the time happened by and gave a quick lesson in table-setting. With a passion for excellence and a lack of institutional savvy, the group operated very differently than most restaurateurs of the time . . . buying fresh produce from local grocers, baking fine pastries from scratch, playing soothing, classical music and offering attentive, benevolent service.

The time was right, and the Ovens of Brittany took Madison by storm. Soon a second dining room was opened to meet the clamor for more *cassoulet, bouillabaisse* and *legumes varies.* But what people really *raved* about was the baking, especially a buttery, crescent-shaped roll that had a name difficult to pronounce. Croissants were an immediate and huge hit, so popular in Madison that the Ovens sold a croissant T-shirt, complete with illustration and pronunciation guide. While the Ovens can lay claim to introducing croissants to the Midwest (indeed, they were one of the first nationwide to serve them), no one had any idea back then just how tremendously popular the flaky roll was to become.

The Ovens' creative "flour children" weren't content with just the discovery of a French classic; it wasn't long before someone got the idea to use the many-layered croissant dough in other ways. The birth of the Morning Bun occurred one day when a clever baker sprinkled cinnamon-sugar onto a long swatch of croissant dough, rolled it, cut it into large rounds, baked them and then rolled the giant, warm buns in more cinnamon-sugar. As Terry Sowka from the Chicago Sun Times gushed, "Paired with strong coffee, the morning bun transports breakfast to another level of existence . . . Only one other thing is better in the morning than a morning bun." Variations on the theme added pecans, almonds or caramel to the basic recipe. Due to an excess of dough scraps, yet another child of the croissant was born: the Karen bun, shaped like a biscuit and drizzled with an orange honey glaze. An entire line of fine breads and pastries was developed, but none of these enjoyed more favor than the Morning Bun. Over time, daily sales soared into the thousands, with record-setting Sunday brunches and wholesale distribution to two airlines. Eventually, as mock morning buns began to spring up around the city and elsewhere, the name was formally changed to Brittany Bun to distinguish the original from the copies.

For nearly seven years Madison had to be content with a single Ovens location, although a small bakery and a more casual dining setting called the Bakers' Rooms were opened upstairs at the State Street location. Next door, there was also Concordance, a health food store operated by other entrepreneurs of the Phoenix persuasion. Hard times fell when the gifted and eccentric Mrs. Guthrie became ill and eventually left for places unknown. Several employees assumed the bank loan and became owners; in this way many of the ideals of Phoenix about the art of living continued to influence how the Ovens related to its customers, employees and the community.

In 1978 a second Ovens of Brittany was opened on Monroe Street, serving more of what Madison's residents clamored for, the baking. The Ovens on Monroe, smaller and more intimate than its sister on State Street, offered European charm with an informal air. The walls were covered with colorful country scenes painted by Karen McKean, an owner and one of the State Street "originals." While the cuisine here leaned more toward pot pies and omelettes, the pastries were as outrageous as ever, to the delight of Madison's west side. A large retail bakery counter and a burgeoning wholesale business helped spread the word further.

From the beginning, the Ovens emphasized fresh, natural ingredients and made a regular place alongside the *boeuf bourguignon* and leg of lamb for vegetarian dishes, considered by many diners to be the healthier choice. Rich-tasting meatless dishes, fine cheeses, seasonal vegetables served with buttery hollandaise sauce, and the baked goods were welcomed by vegetarians and meat-eaters alike. But by the early 1980's a new way of thinking was hitting the finer restaurants across America as people began to take healthy eating more seriously. Now people were talking about eating lighter, watching fat intake and exercising more. And, with the opening of another new restaurant, the Ovens of Brittany responded again.

The Ovens of Brittany-Shorewood opened on Madison's University Avenue in 1981. Designed in the spirit of Frank Lloyd Wright, the third Ovens had a feeling to match its new cuisine—bright, light and alive. It was a remarkable departure from the dark-wooded European flavor of the first two locations. The huge expanse of an ex-grocery store was converted into multi-leveled dining rooms that took on an open, California look, with gleaming wood, greenery, skylights and a waterfall. Stir-fries, fresh juices, open-face melts and many vegetarian dishes highlighted the menu. The Concordance health food store moved from State Street to the larger location in Shorewood, expanding its selection of natural foods to include fresh produce and baked goods. (The space left downtown when Concordance moved was transformed into an elegant oyster bar named The Magic Flute, another Ovens venture.) Later, the health food craze simmered down (or perhaps settled in); meanwhile, the demand for Ovens's bakery continued to increase. Concordance eventually converted to a retail bakery and though the Shorewood restaurant brought many of the older favorites back to the menu, they continued to feature exciting fare for the health-conscious.

By the time the Shorewood Ovens was operating, a host of restaurants, French and otherwise, had opened around Madison in the wake of the Ovens' success. The Ovens became known as the mother of Madison's culinary scene. While naming all the places influenced by the Ovens of Brittany would be unwieldy, it's a point of pride to note some of the flourishing businesses that have been started by people who have worked at the Ovens. Some, like L'Etoile, the Wilson Street Grill, and Capitol Brewery have become Madison landmarks in their own right. Other innovative spin-offs include the Wild Iris Cafe, Monty's Blue Plate Diner, La Brioche Bakery, The Blue Marlin, and Botticelli's.

But the story is getting a bit ahead of itself. By 1984 the three Ovens of Brittanys were part of a much improved dining scene in Madison. Most of the prime eateries, however, were located near the Capitol and on the west side. Hungry adventurers on the less trendy east side were surprised and delighted when the Ovens "did it again" with the opening of the Ovens of Brittany at Camelot Square on Fordem Avenue.

This restaurant was yet another version of Ovens ingenuity, different from the others and yet the same. With four dining rooms on two floors, the east side Ovens had what one newspaper writer described as "the look of an 1880's Paris salon, with lace curtains over Palladian windows, heavy oak woodwork, marble tabletops and gilded wallpaper." The Victorian feeling was comfortable yet elegant and the menu combined eclectic dishes like Danish sandwiches and Belgian beef carbonnade with more standard fare, as well as vegetarian choices and the ever popular breads and pastries. "Ovens East," as it became known, was the first Ovens to be built from the ground up and housed the largest Ovens bakery to date. Management involved customers in the restaurant in new ways, vigorously seeking patron feedback on food and service, planning special events and instituting a money-back guarantee of customer satisfaction.

Besides housing the largest Ovens bakery to date, the east side location also developed an extensive catering menu and soon demand forced the catering operation to move to its own quarters downtown. Stationed in the all-glass First Wisconsin Bank Building on the Capitol Square, the Ovens of Brittany Cafe and Catering serves fast-but-fine food in a cafeteria setting on weekdays and also manages a full-scale catering business.

It would be difficult to locate a corner of Madison not touched in some way by the Ovens of Brittany. Likewise, the menus, the ambiance and the people of the Ovens reflect Madison's own uniquely contrasting qualities. Bernard Pacyniak from Bakery Magazine put it this way: "Like the city itself—Madison retains official airs as a state capital while simultaneously letting its hair grow long as a university town—Ovens of Brittany manages to blend some very traditional values with some very progressive philosophies and ideals."

The Ovens' blend continues to serve it well. Offshoots have sprung up outside the home city in places like Middleton, Wisconsin, where the Ovens Cafe and Grille is housed at the World Trade Center and features grilled fresh fish, seafood and chicken. The quaint town of Mineral Point in southwestern Wisconsin draws tourists to its historical mining attractions and to the dining pleasures of the Ovens of Brittany, part of a bed and breakfast inn called the Chesterfield. During summers, the Ovens serves picnic fare to Shakespeare fans at the renowned outdoor American Players Theatre in Spring Green. Located in Wisconsin but loved throughout the Midwest, the Ovens of Brittany has also gained national recognition in publications such as *The Washington Post, Gourmet,* and *Midwest Magazine.*

Ovens Spirit and Ovens People

Over the past twenty years the evolution of the Ovens' style and cuisine has corresponded to an explosion of interest in fine foods throughout the nation. Our menus have been continuously updated as creative cooks and bakers fine tune customer favorites and develop new delights. Some of what we do is very "in," some is on its way "in", and some is simply "us." Though our earliest and strongest culinary influences have been continental, our spirit, like the country's, is that of the melting pot.

Today, the Ovens offers a little something for everyone in style as well as cuisine: hearty, homey foods like thick, creamy soups and giant muffins; elegant fare like Tournedos Henri or Queen of Sheba Torte; French classics like omelettes and croissants; trendy dishes with exciting "new" ingredients; regional favorites from the Cajun bayous or the southwestern desert; fresh fruits and bountiful stir-fries and salads for the health conscious; and good ol' American home-cooking like meatloaf and fried potatoes. With eclectic menus and distinct designs, each restaurant offers customers a break from the repetitive offerings of most chains.

In fact, the Ovens of Brittany began to identify itself as a chain only a few years ago. Though ownership and management is now consolidated under one board of directors, each restaurant was separately developed, opened, owned and managed by small, overlapping groups of people, most of whom had worked their way up through the ranks of another Ovens operation. Through the years these key people provided the continuity and creativity that gave the restaurants their strong identity of quality and culture, of "different yet the same." So, whether the diner's mood is herbal tea and buttered scones or champagne and wedding cake, the Ovens is where people go for something really special.

The story of the Ovens wouldn't be complete without talking a bit more about all the folks who have made it happen. From the beginning, people were the focus as much as the food. Perhaps this is why the Ovens gained a reputation for attracting talented, exceptional people. The original Phoenix vision was a catalyst for the Ovens; it was many subsequent employees who sustained that vision, developed it and allowed the company to grow and change. An incredible amount of ingenuity, dedication and hard work have gone into the making of the Ovens of Brittany.

Alice Waters, American culinary pioneer and founder of Chez Pannisse restaurant, once pointed out that restaurants are communities. In the fullest sense that is surely an apt description of what the Ovens has been and is to so many of us: a group of people working together, having common interests, common goals, actively participating in achieving those goals. Community is getting through the rough times . . . the hectic Sunday brunches, the "killer" holiday seasons, the clash and clang of a noisy, snowed-under dishroom. Community is also sharing the fun times, the awards, the pride of being involved in a whole greater than the sum of its parts. Credit goes to all the "parts:" every dishwasher, every cook, every baker, "waitron," clerk, every employee who made or makes it more than a job, more than a restaurant, but rather a community.

And none of it could be possible without the support of the larger community. Our customers, loyal, honest and most of all, *hungry,* are very much a part of the Ovens community. From budget-conscious students to affluent professionals, old and new, they are also a part of our history, shaping and forming the organization as much as anything else.

The original Phoenix group viewed the first Ovens of Brittany as a model for positive cultural change. A great deal has changed in the world and at the Ovens since 1972. Today the Ovens no longer tries to teach, but simply to serve its customers. On the other hand, the early values of beauty, service and quality have remained important through much change and growth. The Ovens "caught the wave of the time, of the city," says David Yankovich, an early Phoenix member and ex-owner. "So much in life is mediocre. The Ovens offers a sense of promise, something above and beyond what is normal, what is everyday. It reaches something hidden in our unconscious. It really touches people."

The Ovens Cookbook

I wrote this cookbook because the Ovens has touched me too. I've been involved in three of the restaurants, mostly as chef and manager. The recipes as well as the people of the Ovens have been part of my life for ten years. I've been in close contact with customers, planning their weddings, business meetings, and other special events. I've hawked Chocolate Cadillac Cookies to hungry patrons at outdoor fairs and delivered croissants at 4:30 a.m. in a snowstorm. I've researched medieval recipes for an annual holiday feast, labored on box-lunch assembly lines, and yes, I've even cleaned out the grease trap.

But my first love is cooking, and cooking is why I came to the Ovens. Cooking, like writing, is not wholly satisfying until one's creation is shared, and hopefully, appreciated. Nothing in my years with the Ovens has given me more pleasure than knowing that people really enjoy and appreciate what we cook and serve. This cookbook is another means to share the pleasures of the Ovens of Brittany. It's a way to respond to the many requests we've had over the years for Ovens' recipes, secrets and stories. This book is an attempt to preserve our roots and take stock of what we've accomplished. It's a salute to the very special, very committed people who have made it happen. It's a means to "remember" the Ovens and for customers, old and new, to bring a little of it home with them.

Choosing the recipes was not as easy as I had thought it would be, for there are so many good ones! I tried to include a cross-section of favorite dishes collected throughout the years, covering the spectrum of style and mood at all the Ovens establishments. Low-fat, healthy choices as well as the most sinfully rich, for-your-mental-health-only desserts and dishes are represented. Recipes were written for home cooks with average culinary skills and were double tested, first by someone with professional training and familiarity with Ovens food (me) and second, by home cooks in their own kitchens (my generous friends and family). Some recipes are time consuming; some take only minutes to prepare. I included a chapter called "Terms and Techniques" to offer tips about cooking and to explain some of the special methods used at the Ovens.

You'll find many of the most popular and delicious Ovens dishes in this book, some current and some no longer being served. Most recipes have changed over time, and I generally included the most recent versions of those; but please note, Ovens recipes continue to evolve, and some are prepared differently at each restaurant.

Since there were twenty years worth of recipes from which to choose, I hope my readers will understand if a personal favorite of theirs is missing. Some may find the omission of the Brittany Bun (the original morning bun) disappointing, but its secrets are now being protected. (Never mind, they take two days to make, anyway!) Many other well-loved Ovens recipes are revealed, some for the first time.

A couple of notes: First, about authenticity. If your goal in cooking these recipes is to be assured of the real thing, the essential "Ovens taste," follow the recipes exactly. If, however, you are watching fat intake, if your cupboard holds walnuts instead of almonds, or if you are the kind of cook I am, the kind who can never leave a recipe to its own devices, feel free to substitute or experiment. As California chef Paul Bertolli says, "The danger in any cookbook is that it be slavishly followed at the expense of the enjoyment that comes in being engaged in the process of cooking." Some of the recipes were written with that in mind; some were created from inspired trial-and-error, or just from the simple need to use up leftovers. In many cases, I included suggestions for substitutions or indicated where they might not be appropriate.

Unless otherwise indicated in the recipes, flour refers to the all-purpose, unbleached kind. The word "divided" is used in a recipe's list of ingredients when the item is used in more than one place in the recipe. The total amount of the ingredient to be used is given in the ingredient list, as in "two cups flour, divided."

When I first began talking about doing this cookbook, I asked customers to tell me what phrases or pictures came to mind when they thought of the Ovens of Brittany. Some responses were universal ("croissants," "gourmet," "special," "warm, elegant," "fresh," "delicious," "good feelings"). Others evoked more individual experiences ("the rich aroma of coffee," "the spiral staircase," "comforting, trustworthy," "a bowl of steaming soup," "big baskets of bread," "a chocolate-spattered apron"). One woman responded very simply by describing the Ovens as where she went when she wanted to treat herself. "I deserve it," she said. I liked that one. The Ovens *is* a treat. Here's to treating ourselves.

Terms and Techniques

"All things require skill but an appetite," claimed George Herbert in 1640, but just how much skill is required is a question often faced in the kitchen. Although the dishes in this book come from professional kitchens, the recipes were written for the home cook with an average amount of culinary knowledge. This chapter discusses foods and cooking terms used at the Ovens of Brittany and may be helpful to those of you a bit wary of attempting "professional" cooking. It's also offered to any "foodies" who enjoy reading and talking about food, as much as cooking and eating it!

The Butter Decision: Sweet or Unsalted (Or Margarine)?

Wherever butter is called for throughout this book, unsalted or "sweet" butter is recommended. Though salted butter or margarine may be substituted, it is a matter of personal preference. The Ovens chooses unsalted butter for many of its recipes because of its superior flavor; unsalted butter is sweeter and usually fresher than salted butter and is significantly better tasting than margarine. It's also obviously better for people on a low-salt diet. For those of us watching our cholesterol levels, the controversy over margarine vs. butter rages on, with some research showing that margarine may be no better, and in fact, worse than butter in the fight against cholesterol. There are some concerns about butter containing more pesticide residues than margarine, and butter is more expensive, but we use it whenever that genuine, buttery "Ovens" flavor is preferred.

Cutting fat intake is a good idea no matter what our taste preferences or cost and health concerns. Though many of the Ovens recipes include butter, heart-healthy choices are also an important part of our menus. At home or in restaurants, it's up to each of us to decide what kind and how much fat will be included in our diets.

Chicken Breast Preparation

Customers often comment on the moistness and tenderness of the chicken breasts in dishes featured on Ovens of Brittany menus. There are no deep, dark secrets to proper chicken breast preparation, but there are one or two procedures to follow if you want to be guaranteed juicy, fork-tender chicken.

First, pull or cut off all fat globules. (After all, part of the reason you're buying chicken breasts is for their low-cholesterol content. So get all the fat off.) Place the meat on a cutting board or waxed paper and, with the heel of your hand, pound and flatten the thicker parts of the breasts until they are of uniform thickness. The chicken will now cook more quickly and evenly. To help lock moisture in during the cooking process, dredge the chicken in seasoned flour (see page xvi) and shake off the excess. To sauté, make sure the butter is very hot before adding the chicken and do not crowd the pan. Most important of all, do not overcook the chicken, for it will take only a few minutes on each side with this method. Any further cooking will toughen it. Have your sauce made ahead of time, or remove the chicken breasts from the pan and keep them warm while you finish the sauce in the pan. This method is followed in several recipes in this book, but you can also use it when you are creating your own plain or fancy chicken breast dishes.

Clarified Butter

Clarified butter is butter that has been melted down so that the milk solids in it separate from the clear butter. Milk solids burn at a much lower temperature than pure butter; therefore, when you cook at high heat with whole butter, it will burn easily. When milk solids are removed from butter, the clear yellow liquid, or clarified butter, that remains can be used in cooking methods that call for high heat, such as sautéing.

To clarify butter, slowly melt any amount of whole butter over very low heat. Do not allow it to boil. When it is completely melted, skim off the foamy white substance that has collected on the surface of the butter. Take your time and do not jar the pan unnecessarily. Carefully ladle out the clear yellow butter. There will be a small amount of a thin, milky substance left on the bottom. Both this, and the foamy white milk solids may be discarded, or may be used to add flavor to soups, sauces, vegetable dishes, etc. The clear butter can be used immediately for sautéing or can be stored in the refrigerator for up to two weeks. For each stick (8 tablespoons) of butter, this method will yield about 7 tablespoons of clarified butter.

Creams: Heavy, Whipping, Light and Half-and-Half

Why do some recipes call for heavy cream and some for light cream? Can whipping cream be used interchangeably with heavy cream? Is half-and-half really cream? If you've ever been confused about cream, here's some information that may help.

First of all, creams are differentiated by their butterfat content. In order for a cream to be designated as the "whipping" type, it must have a fat content of at least 30 percent. Containers labeled "whipping cream" are usually from 30 to 35 percent butterfat, while heavy cream has a fat content of 36 to 40 percent. The higher the fat content, the better a cream will whip (at least up to a certain point) and the better it will stand up to high heat without curdling. And creams with higher butterfat content also taste richer.

For these reasons, heavy cream can always be substituted when a recipe calls for creams with a lower fat content and there will be no negative results in the cooking process, (although in baking there will be textural differences). Heavy cream does add richer flavor, but it also adds the extra fat we are sometimes trying to cut down on, and it is more expensive, so the decision to substitute heavy cream is up to you. However, substituting creams with lower fat contents when a recipe calls for heavy cream is not as reliable as the other way around. For example, whipping cream, under the right conditions (see below), will whip to a fluffy foam but may not stand up as well as heavy cream when used in high-temperature cooking.

Light cream usually has a fat content of about 18%; it is most often used in coffee or tea. Half-and-half, on the other hand, with a fat content of about 10 to 12%, cannot legally be called cream at all. It is used, however, as a creamer for coffee or tea, or in soups or sauces, to add a richness that milk can't provide, but at a lower cost than heavier creams.

A special note: Dairy products are pasteurized to kill dangerous microbes and extend shelf life. Ultrapasteurized cream has a longer shelf life than pasteurized cream, but because it is cooked at a higher temperature than standard cream, it has a slightly "cooked" flavor and isn't as reliable when used for whipping or thickening.

To whip cream, keep these principles in mind:

1. Use a glass, ceramic, stainless steel or copper bowl; avoid plastic and aluminum. (Aluminum may react with the cream, turning it grayish in color; and plastic doesn't seem to chill as thoroughly as other materials.)
2. Start with fresh cream. Chill the cream, bowl and beaters thoroughly, for warm temperatures will thin the cream, making it too unstable to create a stiff foam.

3. For maximum volume, add any sugar and flavoring towards the end of the whipping process. White or powdered sugar and vanilla extract are typically used, but other sweeteners and flavorings are optional. Amounts are also up to personal preference.

4. The fluffiness of whipped cream occurs because air is incorporated into the mixture; you can aid the process by moving the beaters up, down and around to allow more air to be incorporated. Stop beating as soon as the mixture forms stiff peaks. Overwhipping will make the whipped cream less stable, or worse, turn it into butter.

Crème Fraîche

Crème fraîche (pronounced krehm fraysh) is similar to sour cream in that it is a cultured cream with a tart flavor, but it has the advantage over sour cream in its ability to stand up to high heat. Thick and tangy, it goes well with fresh fruits, especially berries, and can be found in dressings, dips and sauces. There are many different methods for making this delightful French invention, but this procedure is the simplest and most fool-proof: Whisk until smooth one cup of heavy cream and one cup of sour cream in a glass bowl or bottle. Cover, place in a warm place (top of stove works well) and let stand 12-24 hours, until thickened. Stir, then refrigerate for another 24-36 hours. It will keep up to two weeks. This method yields two cups of crème fraîche. For a tart treat, use it as you would sour or whipped cream.

Croutons

Leftover bread can be turned into culinary treasure by making it into croutons. Cut unused, partially stale bread into bite-sized cubes or cracker-sized shapes. If you don't have the time to cook them immediately, collect them in an open-air container and let them dry out completely. When you get a large enough supply of dried bread, melt butter or heat olive oil and stir in your favorite dried herbs or seasonings (basil, oregano, parsley, garlic powder, tarragon, etc.). Use about 1½ teaspoons dried herbs for each ½ cup of butter or oil. This will coat about 4-5 cups of bread cubes. Toss the bread cubes with the herb-flavored butter or oil (or brush on larger croutons) and spread on a baking sheet. Bake in a preheated 400-degree oven until golden brown, about 8-10 minutes, tossing once or twice during the baking time. Cool thoroughly and store in an airtight container. Homemade croutons add flavor and crunch to salads and soups; larger croutons can replace store-bought crackers and absorb delicious juices under steaks and chops.

Eggs

It's been said that "the egg is to cuisine as the article is to speech," and certainly there are few foods which are as useful and versatile as the egg. In cooking, eggs can enrich, leaven, or be a binding agent; they can provide decoration, texture, nutrition, or flavor. They can stand alone as a satisfying meal in themselves, or blend with other ingredients, savory or sweet. Eggs fit into any meal of the day; it would be very difficult to imagine the culinary world without eggs.

When preparing recipes from this cookbook, use Grade A large eggs. Here is a hodge-podge of thoughts and suggestions about using eggs:

1. Raw eggs, especially those produced on the East coast, may contain salmonella bacteria; recipes that call for uncooked eggs should be avoided. If you are like me and can't resist such delicacies as Caesar salad, then get a guarantee from the store or farmer where you purchase eggs that their product is safe.

2. If you are one of the unfortunate folks with a high cholesterol level, it is a good idea to cut down on egg yolk consumption, but remember that egg whites are cholesterol-free. Two

egg whites may be substituted for one whole egg in many recipes. Or look for egg-white products available today in the grocer's dairy case; they make an excellent substitute for whole eggs, especially in baking. Many nutritionists now say that egg yolks are not quite as bad as we've been told, that moderate consumption (4 to 7 per week) will not raise cholesterol in people who have normal levels of cholesterol. Moderation is the best policy.

3. Please don't overcook hard-cooked eggs! Even a few moments extra can result in a greenish rim around the yolk and a tough, rubbery egg white. Simply cover eggs in cold water in a sauce pan. Bring to a low boil, reduce to a low simmer and set your timer for ten minutes. When the buzzer goes off, drain the eggs and immerse them in ice water to stop the cooking. Keep them in the ice water for several minutes, until completely cooled. Now they will peel easily if you knock them gently and roll them across the kitchen counter. (Note, however, that very fresh eggs do not peel easily.) Peeled hard-cooked eggs can be stored in cold water for several days.

4. An easy way to separate egg whites from egg yolks is to carefully break the whole eggs into a small bowl. Palm up and fingers spread slightly, gently lift the egg yolks out, one at at time, allowing the egg white to fall back into the bowl while the yolk stays in the bend of your fingers. Eggs separate most easily when they are cold.

5. When whipping egg whites, allow them to come to room temperature before you begin beating. This will result in greater volume.

Parmesan Cheese

If you think parmesan cheese is something that comes in a green can, I urge you to buy a chunk of *real* parmesan and try it freshly grated. Fresh parmesan is a hard, grainy cheese perfect for grating, with a texture and flavor that makes it worth the extra expense. A little goes a long way. Grate it finely or into large shavings, or even break off a tiny chunk to nibble on. Just a few shavings make steamed vegetables a real treat; or add it to your next salad and you'll never again think greens are boring. Whenever freshly grated parmesan is called for in this book, it refers to parmesan that one buys in a chunk and grates into larger shavings (unless otherwise noted). If you substitute the fine, pre-grated fresh parmesan found in delis or the dried variety found in cans, be aware that shaved parmesan takes up greater volume than parmesan finely grated; you may wish to cut down on the amount called for.

Parmesan has a low fat content compared to other cheeses, so sprinkle it on soups, scatter it over pizza, and fold it into omelettes, casseroles and many other dishes. You may also want to try other hard Italian cheeses like romano, asiago and pecorino, all delicious cousins of parmesan. You may never go back to that green can again.

Roux

Roux (pronounced roo) is a cooked mixture of flour and fat that is used as a thickening agent in soups, stews, sauces, etc. First the fat (usually butter, as it gives the best flavor) is melted, then flour is stirred in until well combined. The roux is stirred over moderately low heat for a few minutes to cook out the flavor of the raw flour. Sometimes roux is cooked until it begins to brown and acquire a nutty flavor, for use in brown sauces. In Cajun cooking, roux is cooked until it is deep brown, almost black, and gives a smoky, intense flavor. A good roux should be somewhat stiff, not runny. When it has cooled a little, it is added to a simmering liquid (or vice versa) and whisked with a wire whisk until the liquid is free of lumps. Then the liquid, be it soup, sauce, etc., is simmered further (10-20 minutes) until no starchy flavor remains. Roux, unlike cornstarch, is very stable and the thickened sauce or soup will not thin out as it continues to cook.

Sauté

Many people confuse sautéed food with food that is pan-fried or stir-fried. To sauté means to cook quickly over moderately high heat in a small amount of fat, usually butter. Pan-frying involves more butter or oil, more time, and less heat. Stir-frying, on the other hand, cooks small, uniform pieces of food tossed over very high heat in a small amount of oil, never butter.

There are two important things to note about the sauté method: the butter in the pan must be very hot before adding the food to it, and the pan must not be crowded, otherwise the food will simmer, not sauté.

Seasoned Flour

Seasoned flour is simply flour to which salt and pepper, or other herbs and seasonings, have been added. The flour mixture is then used as a coating for foods to be sautéed, pan-fried or deep-fried. You will find seasoned flour called for in several of the recipes in this book. Foods like chicken breasts are dipped in seasoned flour, the excess is shaken off, and the chicken is immediately added to the heated pan. Including seasoned flour in the cooking method adds flavor, crispness and color to the product. The flour coating also helps keep the food from sticking and from absorbing too much fat from the pan. Finally, the flour also helps thicken the sauce, if one is made in the same pan.

To prepare 1 cup of seasoned flour, simply toss 1 cup of flour with 1 teaspoon or more of each salt and pepper. Dried herbs may also be added; they add more flavor and flecks of color to the cooked item. Larger amounts can be made, stored in an airtight container and used whenever needed.

Stock

Stock is the flavor foundation for soups, stews, and sauces. It's a clear, unthickened liquid that results from extracting in water the essence of meat, poultry, fish and their bones, and/or vegetables and seasonings. Culinary stock, like monetary stock, is a valuable investment, for it is easy to make and tastes terrific, adding a low-fat richness to dishes that people really notice. It's what you taste when you notice that a soup seems homemade or a sauce tastes extra special. Stock can be made in large or small amounts, uses ingredients that cost next to nothing, and takes little or no attention. It can be frozen in small containers and used whenever recipes call for water or broth. Stock-making can be extremely simple, as easy as covering bones or vegetables with water and simmering them for an hour, or it can involve more ingredients, more time, and greater attention to things like skimming the surface and clarifying the liquid.

Some stock-making tips: Start with cold water; as it heats, it slowly extracts flavor from bones and other ingredients. Browning the bones first adds color and flavor to the finished product, but is not necessary. Vegetables like broccoli and cauliflower that acquire strong flavor when cooked for a lengthy period should be avoided. Small amounts of herbs or seasonings are used to give subtle flavor. Salt, however, is never used while the stock is cooking; add it later, when the stock is used in a recipe.

Although it's not necessary to follow a precise recipe to make stock, here is a list of the ingredients most often selected. Choose the ingredients according to what type of stock you wish to make . . . chicken, beef, vegetable or fish. Basic stock-making methods follow.

Stock Ingredients:

Chicken, beef, veal or fish bones, preferably raw

Cold water

Vegetable ends or chopped vegetables (celery, carrots, onions and leeks preferred)

Whole peppercorns
Bay leaves (except in fish stock)
Fresh parsley stems (if available)
Dried herbs (parsley, thyme, sage, rosemary, chervil, etc.)

Stock-making Method:

1. Brown bones and/or vegetables in oven or in pan with small amount of oil on top of stove (optional step). Place them in large pot with remaining ingredients; for every quart of bones use about 1 cup of vegetables, 2 or 3 peppercorns, ½ bay leaf, a few parsley stems and about a teaspoon of dried herbs. (If you're making vegetable stock use the same amount of seasonings for every 4-6 cups of vegetables.)
2. Cover the ingredients with cold water. Bring to a simmer, skim the surface and simmer over low heat. Vegetable and fish stocks will take 30-60 minutes, while chicken stock should cook 3-4 hours and beef stock even longer than that if possible. Add more water (hot this time) as the liquid reduces, so that the solids remain covered.
3. When done, strain through cheesecloth or a fine mesh strainer. Discard the solids and, if you've made meat stock, chill the liquid, then remove and discard the fat layer that has formed on the top. Strained stocks may be boiled and reduced to concentrate flavor. A meat stock which has been reduced until syrupy is called a glaze. Stock may be kept several days in the refrigerator or frozen.

Vinaigrette

Vinaigrette is a French term for a dressing made by whisking oil, vinegar (or other acidic liquids) and flavorings together until the mixture is thickened, or emulsified. The ratio of oil to vinegar is usually three or four to one; other flavorings such as mustard, herbs or pressed garlic are added to taste. To prepare a vinaigrette that won't separate quickly, mix all ingredients except the oil. Then, using a wire whisk, beat in the oil in a very thin stream until all of it has been added. Continue to beat for another few minutes.

(If your mixture has egg yolks in it, the dressing will not break down. This is because egg yolk will coat the tiny droplets of oil and vinegar that have formed from all the whisking, and the coating holds the droplets in suspension, creating a permanent emulsion. This same principle applies to the making of mayonnaise.)

Don't confuse vinaigrette, a French dressing, with American French dressing, which follows a similar method but has a specific tomato-onion flavor and a bright red color that comes from its catsup content.

You can easily make delicious, homemade dressings by following the above method and varying the ingredients to suit the season or your preference.

Ovens of Brittany

APPETIZERS
& SOUPS

Stuffed Mushrooms
24-30 mushrooms

There's something about stuffed mushrooms that makes them the first to disappear on an appetizer platter (right after the shrimp cocktail, that is). People must instinctively know that they are at their very best when piping hot. At Ovens of Brittany weddings and catered events, Stuffed Mushrooms are often a buffet choice. From the dozens of possible fillings, here are two popular selections, one made with spicy Italian sausage and the other a vegetarian alternative. When these hot and tender morsels emerge from the oven, we defy you to eat just one!

Sausage Filling:
- ½ pound hot Italian sausage
- 1 teaspoon fennel seeds (optional)
- 2 tablespoons minced celery
- 2 tablespoons minced onion
- ½ teaspoon dried basil
- ½ teaspoon dried parsley flakes
- ⅛ teaspoon red pepper flakes
- ¼ cup breadcrumbs
- ½ cup grated gruyere or Swiss cheese

Heat skillet and brown meat with fennel, breaking up sausage as it browns. Remove mixture with slotted spoon to a bowl. Add celery, onion and herbs to skillet; cook until soft. Combine with the meat, breadcrumbs and cheese. If desired, chop mixture further for a smoother texture.

Vegetarian Filling:
- Stems from 1 pound large mushrooms
- 2 tablespoons olive oil
- 4 tablespoons minced onion
- ½ cup minced celery
- 1 teaspoon dill weed (or dried herb of your choice)
- ½ teaspoon dried parsley flakes
- ⅛ teaspoon red pepper flakes
- 1 cup grated gruyere or swiss cheese

Mince mushroom stems. Heat oil in skillet and sauté mushrooms with onions and celery over fairly high heat, stirring often. When vegetables are tender and moisture has evaporated, lower the heat, add herbs and cook a minute longer. Let mixture cool a bit, then stir in cheese.

To Stuff and Cook Mushrooms:
   1 pound large mushrooms (about 24-30), stems removed
   1 recipe Sausage or Vegetarian Filling

Preheat oven to 450 degrees; grease a baking pan. Heap filling into mushroom caps and place in pan. Bake 10-15 minutes. Serve hot.

Artichokes Parmesan

Serves 4

Here's a simple but sophisticated appetizer that works well as part of an antipasto platter or as a first course. Arrange the hot artichokes on curly lettuce leaves with a few cured olives and a small wedge of lemon.

   2 jars (each 6½ ounces) marinated artichoke hearts
   ½ teaspoon minced garlic
   ⅛ teaspoon ground black pepper
   ⅓ cup fine breadcrumbs
   ⅓ cup finely grated fresh parmesan cheese
   1 egg

Preheat oven to 350 degrees; grease a baking pan. Drain artichokes; cut larger ones in two. Mash garlic and pepper with a fork until a paste forms; mix with breadcrumbs and cheese. In a separate bowl, mix egg and one teaspoon water. Dip each artichoke piece first into egg mixture, then roll it in breadcrumb mixture and place on pan. Bake 15 minutes. Serve immediately. (Frilled toothpicks will make the hot artichokes easy to handle.)

"The kitchen is a country in which there are always discoveries to be made."
—Grimod de la Reyniere, *Almanach des Gourmands,* 1804

Scallops Arienne
Serves 4

A classy, chilled appetizer of creamy scallops with a mustardy tang. It can also be served on a bed of shredded lettuce as a salad.

> 1 pound fresh bay scallops
> Salt and pepper
> ¼ cup dry white wine
> Juice and whole rind of ½ lemon
> ¼ cup Dill Mustard Sauce (page 64)
> 3 tablespoons chopped green onion
> Lettuce leaves
> Ground paprika
> Lemon wedges

Season scallops with salt and pepper. Combine one quart water and the wine in pot and bring to a boil; add lemon juice and rind. Lower heat, add scallops and poach them in very gently simmering water until just tender, about 2-3 minutes. Drain, discard lemon rind, and chill scallops. Fold in Dill Mustard Sauce and green onions. Arrange on lettuce leaves; sprinkle with paprika. Lemon wedges add a bright and tangy touch. This may be served on individual plates or on a small platter with toothpicks available.

Spinach-Stuffed Greek Pastries
Makes 25-30 pastries

Paper-thin phyllo dough is used in this Greek-style appetizer. If you haven't worked with it before, don't be shy! With just a little practice you'll be turning out perfect little triangles stuffed with spinach, parmesan and feta cheese. Believe me, I know! I was once asked to demonstrate this specialty on television's "P.M. Magazine." If I can do it (with the cameras rolling), so can you!

Keep these easy rules in mind: Thaw the dough slowly in the refrigerator ahead of time and don't take it out of the package until ready to use. Have all utensils and ingredients ready and close at hand before you begin the assembly. Use a clean damp towel to cover the exposed dough while you are folding the pastries. Don't worry about rips in the sheets of dough; the many layers hide flaws neatly. And have fun!

> 1 pound box phyllo dough, thawed 24 hours in refrigerator
> 1 pound fresh spinach, cleaned, de-stemmed, cooked briefly, and chopped *OR* 1 box (10 ounces) frozen chopped spinach, thawed
> ½ pound feta cheese, crumbled
> 4 ounces (about 1 cup) freshly grated parmesan cheese
> 2 eggs, lightly beaten
> ½ teaspoon nutmeg
> ½ teaspoon ground black pepper
> ¼-½ pound butter, melted

1. To make filling: drain spinach and squeeze out as much liquid as possible. Combine with feta, parmesan, eggs, nutmeg and pepper.
2. To assemble pastries: have ready the melted butter, a pastry brush, a sharp knife, a slightly damp towel, the filling, the dough, and a large ungreased baking sheet.
3. Carefully unfold dough on large work surface. Pull off two sheets; place together on table with long edge facing you. Brush pastry surface lightly with butter, emphasizing the edges (it's not necessary to cover every inch of dough surface). Pull off another single sheet of dough, place over the others and brush again with butter. Do this twice more, for a total of five sheets. If a sheet rips, patch it if you can but don't be fussy about it. Work quickly to avoid drying out dough. At this point you can place damp towel over the exposed remaining dough.
4. Cut brushed layers vertically into 6 equal strips. Place heaping tablespoon of filling at bottom of each strip. Fold up each strip like a flag: starting at bottom near filling, fold dough over filling to form a triangle and continue to fold triangle back and forth up the strip. Place each folded triangle on baking sheet.
5. Continue this process until all filling is used up; lightly brush stuffed pastries with butter. At this point you may refrigerate or freeze them until ready to use. (Once frozen the pastries may be stacked.)
6. To cook: preheat oven to 375 degrees and bake pastries 20-30 minutes, until golden brown and sizzling hot. (Frozen pastries should be thawed at least partially and will take longer to heat.)

Tomato Dill Soup

Serves 8-10

This is such a pretty soup, with a vivid red color and flecks of green herbs. We make it often because it seems to go with everything (and our customers are always asking for it). The rich taste and texture make it perfect as a first course to an important dinner, but try it with some Bailey's Corn-Oat Muffins (see page 96) for a Monday night supper. Don't worry about leftovers: Tomato Dill Soup tastes even better the second day, and freezes well.

7½ tablespoons butter, divided
½ cup flour
1 cup diced onions
1 large clove garlic, minced
4 cups chicken stock
1 can (29 ounces) tomato puree (or two 15-ounce cans)
1 can (16 ounces) whole peeled tomatoes, chopped, juices reserved
3 tablespoons honey
1 tablespoon dill weed
1 teaspoon basil
½ teaspoon ground black pepper
½ teaspoon chili powder
⅛ teaspoon ground red (cayenne) pepper
3 dashes hot pepper sauce
Salt and pepper to taste

1. To make roux, melt 4½ tablespoons butter in small saucepan. Stir in flour until well blended. Cook over low heat, stirring often, for 3-5 minutes. Remove from heat and set aside.
2. Melt remaining 3 tablespoons of butter in large, heavy pot. Add onions; cook gently 5 minutes. Add garlic; cook two minutes more.
3. Add chicken stock, bring to a boil, and reduce to a simmer. Whisk in roux until stock is thickened and smooth.
4. Add remaining ingredients, including juice from canned tomatoes. Simmer 30-45 minutes, stirring often to prevent scorching. This is a thick soup, but you may adjust to your taste by adding more chicken stock. Add salt and pepper to taste.

Turkey Almond Soup
Serves 4-6

Here's an unusual way to use up leftovers from your holiday bird. Though there's no cream in Turkey Almond Soup, it has a smooth texture punctuated with the crunch of almond slivers and mellowed with a very little sweetness from almond paste.

> **5 tablespoons butter, divided**
> **½ cup flour**
> **¾ cup chopped onions**
> **¾ cup chopped celery**
> **1 ½ teaspoons basil**
> **5 cups chicken stock**
> **2-3 tablespoons almond paste**
> **½ cup dry white wine**
> **2½ cups chopped cooked turkey**
> **½ cup sliced almonds, toasted**
> **Salt and ground white pepper to taste**

1. To make roux, melt 4 tablespoons butter in small saucepan. Stir in flour until well blended. Cook over low heat, stirring often, for 3-5 minutes. Remove from heat and set aside.
2. Melt remaining 1 tablespoon of butter in heavy pot. Add onions and celery; cook 5 minutes, then add basil and cook two minutes more.
3. Add stock, almond paste and white wine, bring to simmer and stir until almond paste is competely dissolved. Whisk in roux until mixture is thickened and smooth.
4. Stir in turkey, almonds and salt and white pepper to taste. Simmer 15-20 minutes. Adjust seasonings and serve.

"A watched pot never boils, and an unwatched pot always boils over."
—Popular saying with Ovens of Brittany Cooks

Navy Bean with Ham Soup
Serves 8

Ah, the virtures of beans . . . a high fiber, low-fat content puts them near the top of the list of cholesterol fighters. The added punch of protein and iron makes beans one of the most nourishing foods available. They are easy to grow in your backyard garden and inexpensive no matter where you buy them.

Legumes play a starring role in dishes from around the world, ranging from something as simple and satisfying as our Navy Bean with Ham Soup or in ones as richly complicated as a French cassoulet. Combined with an inexhaustible variety of meats, vegetables, seasonings or side dishes, beans will delight and content you.

> 2 cups navy beans, soaked overnight in cold water
> 4 cups chicken stock
> 6 cups water
> 1 bay leaf
> 2 tablespoons butter
> 1 cup chopped onion
> 1 cup chopped carrots
> ½ cup chopped celery
> 1 can (16 ounces) whole peeled tomatoes, chopped, juices reserved
> 8 ounces (about 1½ cups) chopped ham
> 2 teaspoons basil
> ¼ teaspoon ground black pepper
> 1/16 teaspoon red (cayenne) pepper
> 2 dashes hot pepper sauce
> Salt to taste

1. Drain and rinse beans. Place in soup pot with chicken stock, water and bay leaf. Bring to a boil, skim surface, then reduce to a strong simmer and cook, uncovered, until beans begin to get tender, about 1 to 1½ hours.
2. Meanwhile, melt butter in a pan and sauté onions, carrots and celery until almost tender. When beans are almost tender, add the cooked vegetables and remaining ingredients (including juice from tomatoes) to pot. Continue to cook 20-30 minutes until beans are very tender.
3. With a large spoon, press beans against sides of pot so that they break up and thicken the soup. Do this with about one quarter of the beans. Taste and adjust seasoning.

Helpful hint: There is one "side effect" of eating beans that discourages some of us. To help prevent this small problem, be sure to soak the dried beans in plenty of cold water overnight, then drain, rinse and cover with fresh water or stock to cook them. The good news is that the more you eat beans, the less discomfort there will be.

Anna's Spinach Lentil Soup
Serves 10

You've heard the old adage: "Too many cooks spoil the soup." The very opposite may be true in our kitchens, for it's been the creative urge of many cooks that has produced the Ovens' ambitious soup repertoire. Soup shifts are very popular among our seasoned cooks, for this is when they can indulge their own fancies and create original recipes. Some adapt long-standing favorites from home, some find wonderful ways to use up leftovers and others comb the cookbook shelves for new ideas. They say soup is good for one's physical and psychological well-being; I believe this is particularly true when the soup has a little of the individual cook's "soul" in it.

Anna Alberici's recipe for Spinach Lentil Soup is an excellent example of the benefits of the creative process. Anna, as her last name may indicate, specializes in Italian cooking. She's a small woman, and would stand on a red milk crate to stir the ten-gallon batches that she often made of this hearty concoction. Anna's recipe combines fresh spinach with lentils, ham, pasta, garlic, onion and a rich, homemade chicken stock. You will love it.

    1 tablespoon olive oil
    1 cup chopped onion
    2 teaspoons minced garlic
    1 pound lentils, rinsed
    1 ham shank (about 1 pound)
    3 quarts chicken stock, preferably homemade
    4 ounces (about 1 cup) uncooked macaroni
    8-10 ounces fresh spinach, twice rinsed, de-stemmed and chopped
    Salt and black pepper to taste

Heat oil in large soup pot and slowly cook onion and garlic until tender. Add lentils, ham shank and chicken stock, bring to a simmer; cook until lentils are tender (about 1 hour). Remove ham shank and set aside to cool. Add macaroni to soup; cook about 8 minutes. Meanwhile, remove ham from the shank, chop meat and return it to the pot (discard bone). Add chopped spinach; cook another minute or two. Add salt and pepper to taste (if you've used canned stock, salt may not be necessary).

Mexican-Style Three Bean and Three Chili Soup

Serves 8-10

In professional kitchens, creative sparks can be ignited in some of the most unlikely ways. This soup was conceived just before inventory, when every bit of food on restaurant shelves must be counted. One is inspired to use up "odds and ends" to avoid endless recording. A spate of Tex-Mex specials left us with some varieties of beans and peppers, and that's how this Mexican-Style Three Bean and Three Chili Soup was born.

You can crank up the mild bite of this soup by adding more cayenne or jalapeno, and feel free to substitute the kidney beans with black beans or your own favorite. If your grocer doesn't carry banana peppers, try a sweet red or green pepper instead. But don't replace the tortilla chips! They add a salty corn crunch that really makes the soup.

> 1 cup navy beans, soaked in water overnight, drained, rinsed
> 1 tablespoon vegetable oil
> 1 cup chopped onions
> 2 teaspoons minced garlic
> 1 bay leaf
> 1 teaspoon oregano
> 6 cups chicken stock, vegetable stock or water (or a combination)
> 1 small banana pepper
> 1 small jalapeno
> 1 can (16 ounces) whole peeled tomatoes, with juice
> 1 can (16 ounces) dark red kidney beans (undrained)
> 1 can (4 ounces) chopped mild green chilies
> 1 teaspoon cumin
> ¼ teaspoon ground red (cayenne) pepper
> 1 can (16 ounces) refried beans
> ¼ cup chopped fresh coriander (cilantro)
> Salt and ground black pepper to taste
> Tortilla chips

1. Heat oil in heavy soup pot, add onions; cook until tender. Add garlic and cook 1 minute more.
2. Add bay leaf, oregano, stock and drained navy beans, bring to strong simmer and cook until beans are tender and beginning to split (about one hour).
3. Meanwhile, remove and discard seeds from jalapeno and banana peppers. Mince peppers and coarsely chop tomatoes, reserving juice. When beans are cooked, add to them the jalapeno, banana pepper, tomatoes (and juice),

kidney beans (and juice), green chilies, cumin and ground red pepper. Stir in refried beans until no lumps remain. Simmer 15-20 minutes.
4. Add coriander and season to taste with salt and black pepper. Garnish with tortilla chips and serve.

Cream of Broccoli Soup
Serves 4-6

Here's an Ovens of Brittany classic that has been enormously popular since the early seventies. Cholesterol wasn't much of a health concern then so the butter and milk content didn't seem to bother anyone. But whether you use margarine instead of butter or two-percent milk instead of cream, you will find Cream of Broccoli Soup savory and rich-tasting.

6 tablespoons butter, divided
⅓ cup flour
¾ cup finely chopped onions
½ cup finely chopped carrots
½ cup finely chopped celery
2 cups coarsely chopped broccoli stems and tops
1 teaspoon basil
½ teaspoon curry powder
½ teaspoon paprika
½ teaspoon thyme
½ teaspoon celery seed
1 cup milk
1 cup half-and-half
2½ cups vegetable or chicken stock
¼ teaspoon ground white pepper
2 dashes hot pepper sauce
Salt to taste

1. To make roux, melt 3 tablespoons butter in small saucepan. Stir in flour until well blended. Cook over low heat, stirring often, for 3-5 minutes. Remove from heat and set aside.
2. Melt remaining 3 tablespoons of butter in large, heavy pot. Add onions, carrots and celery; cook until they are just beginning to get tender. Add broccoli, basil, curry powder, paprika, thyme and celery seed; cook a few minutes longer. Meanwhile, heat milk and half-and-half together.

3. Add stock to vegetables, bring to a boil, and reduce to a simmer. Whisk in roux until soup is thickened and smooth.
4. Stir in heated milk mixture, white pepper and hot pepper sauce. Simmer 10-20 minutes until flavors have blended but broccoli is not overdone. Adjust seasonings and serve.

Cream of Mushroom Soup

Serves 4

Of all the popular Ovens of Brittany "cream" soups, Cream of Mushroom is perhaps the best. With deep mushroom flavor and a rich, silky texture, it's elegant as a first course and wholesome for lunchtime.

5½ tablespoons butter, divided
⅓ cup flour
½ cup chopped onions
½ cup chopped celery
½ pound (3½-4 cups) sliced mushrooms
3¼ cups chicken or vegetable stock, or combination stock and water
1 teaspoon dried basil OR 1 tablespoon chopped fresh basil
1 teaspoon dried parsley OR 1 tablespoon chopped fresh parsley
1 cup milk
½ cup half-and-half
2 tablespoons dried onion-mushroom soup mix
Salt and ground white pepper

1. Make a roux by melting 4 tablespoons butter in a small saucepan. Stir in flour until well blended. Cook over low heat, stirring often, 3-5 minutes. Remove from heat and set aside.
2. Melt remaining 1½ tablespoons butter in soup pot and slowly cook onions and celery over low heat until tender. Raise heat, add mushrooms and continue to cook 4-5 minutes, until mushrooms are tender.
3. Add stock (or stock and water), basil and parsley. Bring to simmer. Meanwhile, heat together milk, half-and-half, and dried soup mix.
4. Whisk roux into simmering mushroom/stock mixture until smooth. Stir in heated milk mixture; simmer 15-20 minutes. Season to taste with salt and ground white pepper.

Cream of Vegetable Soup
Serves 6-8

The vegetables in this soup may vary with the seasons.

7 tablespoons butter, divided
½ cup flour
1½ cups milk
1 cup half-and half or heavy cream
1 cup chopped onion
⅔ cup chopped celery
⅔ cup chopped carrots
⅔ cup sliced mushrooms
⅔ cup chopped broccoli
1 teaspoon minced garlic
1 tablespoon dried basil
1 tablespoon dried thyme
3½ cups vegetable or chicken stock
¼ cup dry white wine
Salt and ground white pepper to taste

1. To make roux, melt 3½ tablespoons butter in small saucepan. Stir in flour until well blended. Cook over low heat, stirring often, for 3-5 minutes. Remove from heat and set aside. Meanwhile, heat milk and half-and-half (or heavy cream) together in microwave or over low heat.
2. Melt remaining 3½ tablespoons butter in a soup pot, add vegetables, garlic, basil and thyme and cook until almost tender, stirring often.
3. Add stock, bring to a simmer and whisk in roux until liquid is smooth. Whisk in warm milk mixture in 2 or 3 installments. Add wine, simmer 10 minutes. Season to taste with salt and white pepper.

"Beautiful soup, so rich and green,
Waiting in a hot tureen!
Who for such dainties would not stoop?
Soup of the evening, beautiful soup!
Beautiful soup! Who cares for fish,
Game, or any other dish?
Who would not give all else for two
Pennyworth only of beautiful soup!
Pennyworth only of beautiful soup!"
—Lewis Carroll, *Alice's Adventures in Wonderland,* 1865

Irish Potato Chowder

Serves 6

7 tablespoons butter, divided
7 tablespoons flour
1 cup chopped onion
⅔ cup diced carrots
⅔ cup diced celery
1 teaspoon dried basil
1 teaspoon dried parsley
1 teaspoon freeze-dried chives
4 cups vegetable or chicken stock
5 cups peeled, diced potatoes (about 1¼ pounds)
3 cups milk
½ cup sour cream
⅛-¼ teaspoon hot pepper sauce
Salt and ground white pepper to taste

1. To make roux, melt 5½ tablespoons butter in a small sauce pan. Stir in flour until well blended. Cook over low heat, stirring often, for 3-5 minutes. Remove from heat and set aside.
2. Melt remaining 1½ tablespoons butter in a soup pot; add onions, carrots, celery, basil, parsley and chives; cook about 10 minutes.
3. Add stock and potatoes and simmer until potatoes are tender (about 15-20 minutes).
4. Stir in milk; return to simmer and whisk in roux until liquid is thickened and smooth. Simmer 10 minutes, stirring occasionally, then add sour cream, hot pepper sauce and season to taste with salt and ground white pepper.

"Eats first, morals after."
—Bertolt Brecht, *The Threepenny Opera,* 1928

New England Clam Chowder

Serves 6

The addition of sour cream (or sour half-and-half) to a traditional New England chowder brings out the "Wisconsin" in this recipe. Leave the nutritious skin on the scrubbed potatoes, and use the red, waxy type; they will hold up better when reheating the soup.

5 tablespoons butter, divided
⅓ cup flour
1 cup chopped onion
1 pound diced, unpeeled, new potatoes (3 cups diced)
1 tablespoon dried parsley
1 bottle (8 ounces) clam juice
2 cups water or stock (seafood, vegetable, or chicken)
1 cup milk
½ cup half-and-half
2 cans (each 6½ ounces) chopped clams, undrained
½ cup sour cream, at room temperature
¼ teaspoon ground white pepper
2 dashes hot pepper sauce

1. To make roux, melt 4 tablespoons butter in small saucepan. Stir in flour until well blended. Cook over low heat, stirring often, for 3-5 minutes. Remove from heat and set aside.
2. Heat remaining 1 tablespoon of butter in a soup pot. Add onions; cook gently about 5 minutes until tender.
3. Add potatoes, parsley, clam juice and water or stock to pot, bring to a simmer; cook until potatoes are just tender, about 12-15 minutes.
4. Meanwhile, heat milk and half-and-half together gently. Do not boil.
5. When potatoes are tender, add heated milk mixture to pot and return mixture to a simmer. Whisk in roux until liquid is thickened and smooth. Add clams (along with their juice) and heat through.
6. Stir in sour cream, white pepper and hot pepper sauce. Taste and adjust seasonings.

Minestrone

Serves 5-6

This bountiful Italian soup sports a wealth of healthy ingredients but it tastes too good to be good *for* you! Pair a bowl of steaming Minestrone with a hunk of whole grain bread and you'll be in for some indulgent nourishment.

3 tablespoons olive oil
1 cup chopped onion
2 teaspoons minced garlic
⅔ cup chopped carrots
⅔ cup chopped celery
⅔ cup chopped zucchini
½ cup chopped sweet bell pepper (green or red)
½ cup chopped green beans (optional)
2 teaspoons dried basil
1 can (24 ounces) "V8" vegetable juice
2 cups vegetable or chicken stock
1 cup peeled, seeded, chopped tomatoes, fresh or canned
1 can (15 ounces) kidney beans, undrained
4 ounces macaroni or other dried pasta (about 1 cup dried)
2 tablespoons minced fresh parsley
Salt and fresh ground pepper to taste

Heat oil over medium heat in soup pot, add onion, garlic, carrots and celery; cook 5 minutes. Add zucchini, green or red pepper, green beans (if desired) and dried basil; cook 5 minutes. Add vegetable juice, stock, tomatoes, kidney beans; simmer 10-15 minutes. Add macaroni and fresh parsley; cook until pasta is tender, 10-12 minutes. Season to taste with salt and pepper. (An alternative step is to cook macaroni separately and add it to the individual bowls; this way the pasta will not continue to absorb liquid and get mushy as leftover soup cools down.)

Spanish Country Soup

Serves 8

A little smoky, a little spicy, and very substantial, Spanish Country Soup unites sausage, potatoes, ham, tomatoes, spinach and two kinds of beans in a garlicy broth. Soak it up with crusty bread and wash it down with a bracing mug of beer for a stick-to-your-ribs combination.

2 tablespoons olive oil
1 cup chopped onion
2 teaspoons minced garlic
¼ pound diced ham
1½ cups peeled, chopped fresh tomatoes (or use canned)
1 can (19 ounces) garbanzo beans
1 can (15.8 ounces) Great Northern or navy beans
5 cups chicken stock or combination stock and water
1 teaspoon ground cumin
½ pound chorizo sausage or hot Italian sausage
2 cups unpeeled, diced potatoes
½ pound fresh spinach, cleaned and chopped OR 1 package
    (10 ounces) chopped frozen spinach, thawed
Salt and ground black pepper to taste

Heat olive oil in large soup pot; add onions and cook until tender. Add garlic; cook 1-2 minutes. Add ham; cook 2-3 minutes. Add tomatoes, both cans of beans (and their juices), stock (or stock and water), and cumin. Bring to a simmer.

Meanwhile, heat frying pan and brown chorizo or Italian sausage, crumbling meat as it fries. Drain off fat and add browned meat to soup along with the potatoes. Simmer until potatoes are tender, about 15 minutes. Stir in chopped spinach and season to taste with salt and pepper. Simmer 5-10 more minutes.

Chilled Cucumber Yoghurt Soup
Serves 2-4

1 ½ pounds cucumbers
1 container (16 ounces) plain non-fat yoghurt
1 tablespoon cider vinegar
1 tablespoon olive oil
1 teaspoon dried mint *OR* 1 tablespoon chopped fresh mint
1 teaspoon dried dill weed *OR* 1 tablespoon chopped fresh dill weed
¼ teaspoon salt
⅛ teaspoon ground white pepper
½ cup heavy cream or half-and-half

Peel cucumber; slice in half lengthwise and scoop out the seeds. Puree in food processor. Mix with remaining ingredients and chill thoroughly.

Gazpacho
Serves 4-6

A summer without gazpacho is like a movie without popcorn.

1 teaspoon minced garlic
1 teaspoon salt
1 pound fresh tomatoes, peeled, seeded and finely chopped
    (about 2-2½ cups)
1 large green pepper, finely chopped (about 1 cup)
1 medium cucumber, peeled, seeded and finely chopped (about ⅔ cup)
1 small onion, minced (about ½ cup)
1 can (24 ounces) "V8" vegetable juice
3 tablespoons red wine vinegar
3 tablespoons olive oil
2 tablespoons minced fresh parsley
½ teaspoon ground black pepper
½ cup breadcrumbs (optional)

With a fork or the back of a knife, press minced garlic and salt together until they form a paste. Combine with remaining ingredients and chill.

Ovens of Brittany

SALADS &
SALAD DRESSINGS

Chicken Almond Salad
Serves 6-8

There must be a hundred renditions of chicken salad, but this one hits all the right notes. Chunks of tender chicken integrated with cool grapes, almond slivers, celery, red onion, herbed mayonnaise and the zest of fresh lemon juice. The Ovens of Brittany in Shorewood introduced Chicken Almond Salad on their menu and it quickly spread to become a standard at our other locations. For a toasty flavor, be sure to bake the almonds until lightly browned before adding them to the salad.

    1⅓ cups mayonnaise
    1½ tablespoons freeze-dried chives
    2 tablespoons fresh lemon juice
    ½ teaspoon coriander
    ½ teaspoon nutmeg
    ¼ teaspoon ground (cayenne) red pepper
    5-5½ cups chopped cooked chicken
    1½ cups chopped celery
    1 cup halved seedless red grapes
    ¼ cup minced red onion
    Salt and pepper to taste
    ½ cup sliced almonds, toasted (plus additional for garnish)

For garnish:
    Tiny bunches of red grapes
    Toasted sliced almonds

Combine first six ingredients then mix with remaining ingredients except almonds. Refrigerate an hour or two to allow flavors to blend. Stir in almonds, taste and adjust seasoning. Garnish with grapes and more almonds.

"You can put everything, and the more things the better, into a salad, as into a conversation; but everything depends on the skill of mixing."
—Charles Dudley Warner, *My Summer in a Garden,* 1871

Wild Rice Salad
Serves 4-6

Tender, earthy wild rice, crunchy cashews, sweet raisins, oriental vegetables and a citrus-soy sauce dressing with fresh ginger and garlic. Wow! This salad is a joy to make and eat because of its unusual ingredients and intricate flavors. Use a cholesterol-free mayonnaise and you can enjoy the excitement of Wild Rice Salad without any guilt. We can't decide if we like it best just after the components have "met" or once they've gotten to know each other better. Either way, please serve this exceptional rice salad at room temperature for maximum pleasure.

Salad Ingredients:
⅔ cup wild rice
½ cup white rice
¼ cup chopped green onion
2 stalks celery, thin-sliced diagonally
¼ pound snow peas, stringed and cut into 1-inch pieces
½ cup raisins or currants
1 can (8 ounces) sliced water chestnuts, drained
¾ cup cashews, toasted

Dressing Ingredients:
¼-½ cup mayonnaise
2 tablespoons soy sauce or tamari
1 teaspoon freshly grated ginger root
1 teaspoon minced garlic
1 teaspoon finely grated lemon peel
1 teaspoon finely grated orange peel
2 tablespoons fresh lemon juice
2 tablespoons fresh orange juice
2 dashes hot pepper sauce

For Garnish:
Lettuce leaves
Orange wedges

Cook wild and white rices, separately, according to their package instructions. Cool and combine with remaining salad ingredients. Whisk dressing ingredients together until smooth, then toss well with the salad. Serve on crisp green lettuce leaves with bright orange wedges for a garnish.

Apple Walnut Blue Cheese Salad With Raspberry Vinaigrette
Serves 4

Very simple, very different, very good!

   4 cups coarsely chopped romaine lettuce
   2 large tart apples (eg. Grannysmith)
   8 tablespoons chopped walnuts, toasted
   4 ounces blue cheese, crumbled
   ¼-½ cup Raspberry vinaigrette (see below)

Divide the lettuce evenly among four chilled salad plates. Cut apples into large chunks and arrange on the lettuce. Sprinkle on walnuts and crumbled blue cheese, drizzle the dressing over all and serve.

Raspberry Vinaigrette
Makes about 1 ½ cups

The cooks on Monroe Street in Madison were the first to include this berry-based salad dressing on the Ovens' menus. It's light but has a luscious flavor that one can intensify further by adding more raspberries or using raspberry vinegar. You can substitute other types of berries to vary the theme, but you may find that the raspberry reigns in this recipe. Raspberry Vinaigrette makes a plain green salad very special, or can dress up fresh fruit in a summery way. For a very upscale treat, try this dressing on the Apple Walnut Blue Cheese Salad above.

   ½ cup fresh or unsweetened frozen raspberries, thawed
   1 egg or 2 egg whites
   1 ½ tablespoons honey
   ¼ cup apple cider vinegar or raspberry vinegar
   ¾ cup vegetable oil

In blender or food processor puree raspberries, egg and honey. Mix in vinegar thoroughly. With machine running, slowly add oil in a thin stream. Dressing will be thickened and smooth.

State Street Dinner Salad
With Classic Vinaigrette Dressing
Serves 6

This is a very simple but UTTERLY delicious salad. No fancy garnishes or elaborate doodads to dress it up . . . just crisp romaine lettuce, lots of freshly grated parmesan cheese, and plenty of garlicky flavor. Similar to, but lighter than a Caesar Salad, it can be served before or after the main course. Customers at the Ovens of Brittany on State Street have often been seen consuming this salad with a bowl of soup and a warm croissant, a classic meal indeed.

1 very large or two small heads romaine lettuce
1-1½ cups freshly grated parmesan cheese
½-¾ cup Classic Vinaigrette Dressing (see below)
Freshly ground black pepper

Gently wash and chop lettuce. Pat dry (or spin in a lettuce spinner) and wrap in a large clean towel. Refrigerate for ½ hour or longer to "crisp" the lettuce. To serve, toss lettuce with cheese and the desired amount of dressing. Place on chilled salad plates and pass the pepper mill.

Classic Vinaigrette Dressing
Makes 2½ cups

This garlicky dressing also makes a marvelous marinade for vegetables or chicken.

1 teaspoon minced garlic
½ teaspoon salt
2 tablespoons fresh lemon juice
⅓ cup tarragon vinegar
1 tablespoon Dijon-style mustard
1 teaspoon sugar
½ teaspoon ground black pepper
¼ teaspoon ground white pepper
1 egg or 2 egg whites
⅔ cup olive oil
1 cup salad oil

Mash together the garlic and salt until a paste forms. Mix in remaining ingredients except the oils. Whisk in olive oil, then salad oil, in a thin stream.

Concert Curry Chicken Salad
With Pea Pods
Serves 6

Some of Madison's finest moments occur every Wednesday night for six weeks during the summer. Thousands of picnickers are treated to a free open-air concert on the lawn of the Capitol Square. As guests nibble on everything from peanut butter to pâté, the Madison Symphony Orchestra fills the air with the sounds of music. It's a glorious tradition.

Area restaurants compete each year for the pleasure of supplying box lunches to the crowds, and the Ovens of Brittany is a regular participant. Chicken salad of some sort is often packed into the Concert boxes, for it is hard to imagine better picnic fare. Here's a recipe for a lovely Curry Chicken Salad with Pea Pods and other delights.

3½ cups chopped, cooked chicken
1 can (8 ounces) sliced water chestnuts, drained
½ cup chopped green onion
2 chopped hard-cooked eggs
¼ pound snow peas, stringed and cut into 1-inch pieces
½ cup sour cream
½ cup mayonnaise
1 tablespoon lemon juice
½ teaspoon sugar
1 teaspoon curry powder
¼ teaspoon ground ginger
Salt and pepper to taste
Lettuce leaves

Combine all ingredients except lettuce gently but thoroughly. Serve on lettuce leaves. Will keep refrigerated 2-3 days.

Danish Egg Salad
Serves 6

Butter thin slices of dense, dark rye bread and mound this simple egg salad on top for a delicious Danish treat. At one time, the Ovens of Brittany at Camelot Square served a mini-smorgasbord that included small squares of buttered rye bread with several toppings: marinated mushrooms, thinly-sliced roast beef, smoked fish and onions, and Danish Egg Salad. Eyes would light up as this charming assortment of tiny open-faced sandwiches was presented at the table on a round wooden board.

8 eggs, hard cooked
½ cup finely chopped green onions
1 stalk celery, minced
½ cup minced sweet pickles
⅓ cup mayonnaise
½ teaspoon dried dill weed *OR* **2 teaspoons chopped fresh dill**
½ teaspoon black pepper
½ teaspoon salt

Peel and finely chop eggs. Combine gently with remaining ingredients.

"Oh herbaceous treat!
Twould tempt the dying anchorite to eat;
Back to the world he'd turn his fleeting soul,
And plunge his fingers in the salad bowl;
Serenely full, the epicure would say
'Fate cannot harm me—I have dined today.' "
—Sydney Smith, *Recipe for Salad,* 1843

Antipasto Pasta Salad
Serves 6-8

Pasta salads, like any other dishes, are only as good (or as great) as their individual ingredients. In this recipe, using high quality ham and freshly grated parmesan cheese plus a homemade dressing makes all the difference in the world. Dried basil is fine, but try pesto for a fresher, more energetic flavor. And remember, Antipasto Pasta Salad should never be served cold. Time its preparation so you can enjoy it within an hour or so after it is assembled. If you must refrigerate it, bring it back to room temperature before serving.

Salad Ingredients:
> 6 ounces pasta (bowties, corkscrews or your choice)
> 1 tablespoon olive oil
> ½ pound ham or hard salami, minced or julienned
> ½-1 cup freshly grated parmesan cheese
> ½ cup chopped green onion
> 2 tablespoons minced fresh parsley
> 1 can (14 ounces) artichoke hearts, drained and quartered
> ½ cup sliced black olives
> Juice of ½ lemon

Dressing Ingredients:
> 2 tablespoons red or white wine vinegar
> 1 teaspoon Dijon-style mustard
> ½ cup olive oil
> 1 tablespoon dried basil *OR* 1 heaping tablespoon pesto
> Salt and freshly ground black pepper to taste

Garnishes:
> Lettuce leaves
> Cherry tomatoes
> Cucumber slices
> Whole black olives

Cook pasta until just tender in a large amount of boiling, salted water. Rinse with cold water and drain thoroughly, then combine with remaining salad ingredients. To make dressing, mix vinegar and mustard then slowly whisk in ½ cup olive oil. Stir in basil (or pesto), salt, and plenty of freshly ground black pepper. Pour over salad; toss lightly. Serve on crisp lettuce leaves with bright garnishes, like cherry tomatoes, cucumber slices and black olives.

Caesar Salad

Makes 2 main-course salads or 4-6 small salads

If you've never prepared Caesar Salad at home, you've simply got to try it. It's much easier to fix than is commonly believed. And though this classic combination of romaine lettuce, parmesan cheese, croutons and garlic dressing is usually served at the beginning of a meal, there's no reason not to indulge in a whole bowl of it as a main course. It makes a particularly zesty and healthful meal in the heat of summer, when the last place we want to be is slaving next to a hot stove. Round it out with a chunk of french bread and a helping of sliced garden tomatoes.

(If you are absolutely opposed to including anchovies in the dressing, you may substitute ½ teaspoon salt.)

    1 large head romaine lettuce
    1 teaspoon (or more, if you dare) chopped garlic
    1 teaspoon ground black pepper
    2 anchovies *OR* 1 teaspoon anchovy paste *OR* ½ teaspoon salt
    1 egg yolk or egg white
    1½ teaspoons worchestershire sauce
    1½ teaspoons Dijon-style mustard
    1 tablespoon red wine vinegar
    Juice of ½ lemon
    4-6 tablespoons olive oil
    ½-1 cup freshly grated parmesan cheese
    ½-1 cup croutons
    Freshly ground black pepper

Rinse lettuce. Chop into pieces. Dry in salad spinner or in a clean towel. Store in refrigerator until ready to serve. In a large bowl, mash garlic, pepper and anchovies or salt until a paste forms. Mix in egg yolk or egg white, worchestershire sauce, mustard, vinegar and lemon juice. Whisk in oil, adding up to 6 tablespoons to suit your taste. Add lettuce, parmesan and croutons and toss lightly to distribute dressing evenly. Serve on chilled plates and pass the pepper mill.

Tuna Salad With Walnuts

Serves 4

2 cans (each 6½-7 ounces) tuna, packed in water
2 stalks celery, finely chopped
2 tablespoons minced onion
½ cup chopped walnuts
½ cup mayonnaise
1 tablespoon Dijon-style mustard
1 tablespoon fresh lemon juice

Drain tuna and mix well with remaining ingredients. Pile tuna salad in cold sandwiches and on crackers, use to stuff red ripe tomatoes and celery sticks, or mound on bread and broil with cheese for a hot tuna melt.

Tropical Waldorf Salad

Serves 6-8

1½ cups fresh pineapple chunks
3 firm apples (Grannysmith or Golden Delicious or your favorite),
   cut into chunks
1 cup seedless red grapes, halved
½ cup diagonally sliced celery (1 large stalk)
¼ cup plain yoghurt
¼ cup mayonnaise
2 tablespoons honey
1 tablespoon fresh lemon juice
½ teaspoon vanilla extract
1 cup toasted whole or halved nuts (almonds, cashews, walnuts
   or Macadamia nuts)

Combine pineapple, apples, grapes, and celery. In a separate small bowl, stir together the yoghurt, mayonnaise, honey, lemon juice and vanilla. Mix dressing with fruit. Chill. When ready to serve, fold in the toasted nuts.

Marinated Vegetables

There is no precise recipe for this delicious jumble of fresh flavors. You can "mix and match" the ingredients to this salad to fit the season or your taste. Choose 5 or 6 vegetables and use them in roughly equally portions, or again, as desired. You will need about one tablespoon of chopped fresh herbs for every 3 or 4 cups of vegetables. Toss the salad with oil and vinegar or a good vinaigrette dressing, enough to coat the vegetables well. Add salt and freshly ground black pepper to taste. Let the salad marinate several hours in or out of the refrigerator, tossing often. Serve as a first course or to accompany meat, fish or poultry.

Vegetables:
    Green, red, yellow or purple sweet bell peppers, cut into thin strips
    Celery, thin-sliced diagonally
    Thin red onion circles or chopped green onions
    Garbanzo or dark red kidney beans
    Quartered artichoke hearts
    Carrots, thin-sliced diagonally and blanched
    Blanched broccoli flowerettes
    Blanched cauliflower flowerettes
    Cherry tomatoes
    Sliced mushrooms
    Black or green olives, pitted and halved
    Sliced zucchini rounds
    Blanched green or wax beans
Other ingredients:
    Chopped fresh herbs (parsley, dill, thyme, lemon thyme, mint,
      chives, oregano, basil, fennel, tarragon, rosemary, etc.)
    Oil and vinegar or Vinaigrette Dressing (page 23)
    Salt and freshly ground black pepper

"According to the Spanish proverb, four persons are wanted to make a good salad: a spendthrift for oil, a miser for vinegar, a counsellor for salt, and a madman to stir it all up."
—Abraham Hayward, *The Art of Dining,* 1852

Curry Dressing

Makes 1¼ cups

Although there are many similarities in the Ovens of Brittany menus, customers come to all our locations to sample the specialties of each restaurant. When we opened at Camelot Square on the east side of Madison in 1984 we wanted to find a house dressing that was really different. We had pored through endless cookbooks with no real luck. Then one evening a friend served me a salad with an unusual dressing: it had a beautiful creamy yellow color and a slightly sweet, exotic flavor.

She had purchased the dressing at Greenleaf Grocery, a small Madison market that sold high-quality produce and dry goods in bulk. When I visited their deli to find out more about the dressing they were kind enough to let me see the recipe. It seems the secret ingredient was chutney, an East Indian condiment hard to find in those days. We set to work to develop an Ovens version of this unique dressing and the recipe that resulted has been served at Ovens East since opening day. Not only is it a favorite on tossed lettuce greens, we serve it often as a dip for fresh vegetables.

You can find chutney at most large grocery stores, usually in the gourmet section. Make the dressing one day before you plan to use it to allow it to develop color and flavor.

> 1 cup mayonnaise
> 2 tablespoons bottled mango chutney
> 2 tablespoons milk
> 1 tablespoon fresh lemon juice
> 1 teaspoon honey
> 1 teaspoon curry powder
> ¼ teaspoon ginger powder
> ¼ teaspoon garlic powder
> ¼ teaspoon turmeric

Mix all ingredients together in small bowl and refrigerate overnight. Serve on your favorite tossed green salad, or use as a dip for vegetables.

Blue Cheese Dressing

Makes 1¼ cups

A restaurant critic once described this Blue Cheese Dressing as "the real thing" and I think you'll agree . . . it's thick and luscious with plenty of blue cheese flavor. The secret is to blend the cheese with the other ingredients in a food processor or blender and let the flavor develop for several hours. Try this dressing as dip for fresh vegetables or spread it on a roast beef or turkey sandwich.

½ cup sour half-and-half (a lower fat sour cream)
⅓ cup mayonnaise
2 ounces (½ cup crumbled) blue cheese
3 tablespoons milk
1 tablespoon red wine vinegar
⅛ teaspoon salt
⅛ teaspoon ground black pepper

Combine all ingredients in food processor or blender and mix until smooth.

Creamy Garlic Dressing

Makes 1¼ cups

¼ cup sour cream
¼ cup mayonnaise
¼ cup salad oil
1 teaspoon minced fresh garlic
2 teaspoons dried chives OR 2 tablespoons fresh chives
¼ teaspoon white pepper
½ cup buttermilk

Thoroughly mix sour cream and mayonnaise then whisk in oil. Stir in remaining ingredients and refrigerate at least one hour before serving. The garlic flavor will intensify as this dressing ages.

Celery Seed Salad Dressing

Makes about 1 cup

An uncommon variation of common American French dressing.

3 tablespoons catsup
2 tablespoons honey
¼ cup apple cider vinegar
1 ½ teaspoons celery seed
½ teaspoon salt
¼ teaspoon ground black pepper
½ cup salad oil

Blend all ingredients except the oil in a food processor or medium-sized bowl. Leave the machine running while you add the oil in a very thin stream (or whisk it in by hand). Continue to run machine or whisk until dressing is smooth and thickened; it will break down easily if you have not added the oil slowly enough.

Salad Notions

Salad-making beckons the creative juices to flow. Walk through the fresh produce section of a quality market for inspiration. Take a brainstorming tour through your own refrigerator and give your leftovers new life. Or choose any of the salad dressings from this chapter and toss with lettuce, pasta, cooked grains or potatoes, and other edibles. Here are some suggestions to get you beyond croutons and cucumbers:

For added crunch:
    sunflower seeds
    slivered almonds
    cashews or other nuts
    chow mein noodles
    apple bits

For protein:
    garbanzo beans
    kidney beans
    peanuts

For a little saltiness:
    greek olives
    anchovies
    pickles

Instead of bacon bits:
    smoked fish
    grilled vegetables

For sweetness:
    raisins
    dried pineapple bits
    strawberry or melon slices
    nectarine or peach wedges

For added flavor:
    chopped fresh herbs
    capers
    salsa
    mustard
    horseradish

Ovens of Brittany

CHICKEN & BEEF

Chicken Pot Pie
Serves 2-4

Don't let the name fool you! With golden puff pastry crowning tender morsels of chicken breast and vegetables in a creamy herb sauce, Chicken Pot Pie makes a regal feast.

Not a chance you'll tackle puff pastry, you say? No problem, now that there are high quality, reliable versions of this special dough in your grocer's freezer case. It's fun to cut rounds for capping individual baking dishes or top a deep dish pan to serve a single pie. Keep the rest of the meal simple because this one will fill your senses *and* your stomach!

> **5 tablespoons butter, divided**
> **1¼ cups chopped onion**
> **1¼ cups chopped carrots**
> **1¼ cups chopped celery**
> **½ teaspoon thyme**
> **½ teaspoon rosemary**
> **1 bay leaf**
> **1 pound boneless, skinless chicken breasts, cut into small chunks**
> **2 cups chicken stock**
> **½ cup flour**
> **¼ cup half-and-half**
> **½ cup peas, fresh or frozen**
> **Salt and ground white pepper**
> **Frozen, pre-rolled, ready-to-use puff pastry**

1. Melt 1 tablespoon butter in heavy saucepan; add and cook onions, carrots, and celery over medium heat about 3 minutes. Add thyme, rosemary and bay leaf; cook until vegetables are just tender.
2. Add chicken; cook a few minutes until chicken turns white.
3. Add stock, bring to a simmer and continue to cook a few more minutes while you make the roux.
4. To make the roux, melt remaining 4 tablespoons of butter in small saucepan. Stir in flour until well blended. Cook over low heat, stirring often, for 3-5 minutes. Remove from heat; set aside.
5. Strain chicken/vegetable mixture through a colander set over a bowl. Return liquid to the pot and set solids aside. After returning liquid to a simmer, whisk in roux until sauce is thickened and smooth. Simmer 3-5 minutes. Meanwhile, heat the half-and-half (can use pan the roux was in).

6. Stir half-and-half and peas into simmering liquid, then stir in the chicken/ vegetable mixture (with bay leaf discarded). Season to taste with salt and white pepper. Set filling aside while you thaw puff pastry for baking. (Or, if you are not going to bake the pie immediately, refrigerate the filling until ready to use.)
7. Pre-heat oven to 350 degrees. Carefully thaw puff pastry according to package instructions. Roll and cut dough to fit the tops of four oven-proof dishes or one pie pan. Divide filling into dishes or pan. Top filling with dough and make two small slashes with sharp knife in top of pastry.
8. Bake 40-45 minutes, until pastry is puffed high and golden brown. Serve immediately. (*Note:* an alternative to above baking method is to keep filling hot while you cut and bake crust(s) on a greased baking sheet until puffed. This will result in crusts with extra height. No venting slashes are required this way. Then pour heated filling into dishes or pan, place puffed crust on top and serve immediately.)

Variations: Leftover cooked chicken or turkey may be substituted for the raw chicken breast. If you do this, skip Step 2 and add meat with the peas. You may also substitute other seasonal vegetables or herbs for the ones used in this recipe.

"*Jack Sprat could eat no fat,*
His wife could eat no lean,
And so between the two of them
They licked the platter clean."
—Anonymous English proverb

Poulet Parisienne

Serves 6

A very special occasion dish, Poulet Parisienne (pronounced poo-leh pah-ree-zee-ahn) is fantastically rich and delicious. Longtime customers of the Ovens may remember Poulet Parisienne from the old days on State Street. Back then it was made to order, and when you read the recipe, you'll understand why that was such an amazing feat!

Today, you can make Poulet Parisienne ahead of time and simply reheat it before serving. The brandy mushroom cream sauce is flavored with tarragon and contains a rather surprising ingredient . . . catsup! Lightly browned chicken breasts blanketed in the mouth-watering sauce are served over rice.

   10 tablespoons butter, divided
   ⅔ cup minced onion
   1 cup chicken stock, divided
   2½ tablespoons flour
   2 pounds skinless, boneless chicken breasts
   4 tablespoons oil
   1 cup chopped onions
   4 cups sliced mushrooms
   ⅔ cup brandy
   1 tablespoon dried tarragon flakes
   4 tablespoons catsup
   2 cups heavy cream
   1 teaspoon tarragon vinegar
   Salt and ground white pepper to taste
   Cooked white rice or rice pilaf
   Chopped fresh parsley (for garnish)

1. Melt 4 tablespoons butter in small pan, add ⅔ cup minced onion and cook over low heat until tender. Add ⅔ cup chicken stock, bring to simmer and whisk in flour. Stir and simmer until mixture is very thick, about 5-7 minutes. Turn off heat; set aside.
2. Trim chicken breasts of all fat and flatten each with heel of hand. Melt 2 more tablespoons of butter in a large sauté pan. When butter begins to sizzle, brown chicken breasts lightly on each side, then remove to a platter. Repeat with more butter and remaining chicken. Remove chicken from pan and set aside until later (refrigerated, if necessary).
3. In the same pan, heat remaining butter and the oil. Add 1 cup chopped onion; cook gently for several minutes. Raise heat to medium-high, add mushrooms and cook until half done.
4. Lower heat again and pour in brandy (carefully, so it does not flame up) and the remaining ⅓ cup of chicken stock. Bring to a boil and cook until liquid in pan is reduced by about one half.
5. Stir in butter/flour mixture thoroughly, then tarragon and catsup. Add whipping cream, bring to a strong simmer and cook until sauce is well thickened, about 20-30 minutes. Stir in vinegar and season to taste with salt and white pepper.
6. To serve, return chicken to pan and simmer gently until chicken is just tender and cooked through (about 5 minutes). Place chicken breasts on rice or rice pilaf and ladle sauce on top. Sprinkle with chopped parsley.

"Meat is a natural nourishment of man because his stomach is too small to deal with the bulk of food he would have to consume if his diet was restricted to fruit and vegetables."
—Jean-Anthelme Brillat-Savarin, *The Physiology of Taste,* 1825

Chicken Carbonara
Serves 4-6

The sauce in this recipe is a lusty blending of two kinds of bacon, mushrooms, green olives, green onions, garlic, tomatoes, white wine, parmesan and cream. It is heavenly just as is over fettuccine, but the addition of sautéed chicken breasts will make it one of your favorite ways to serve poultry. If you don't have both Canadian and regular bacon, use one or the other.

 1 tablespoon olive oil
 ½ cup chopped bacon (about 4-5 slices)
 ¼ cup chopped Canadian bacon (about 1½ ounces)
 ½ pound sliced mushrooms
 ½ cup chopped green onions
 2 teaspoons minced garlic
 ⅔ cup chopped fresh or canned tomatoes
 ½ cup sliced stuffed green olives
 ½ teaspoon thyme
 ½ teaspoon oregano or marjoram
 ¼ teaspoon ground black pepper
 ½ cup dry white wine
 2 tablespoons flour
 ¾ cup heavy cream
 ¾ cup half-and-half
 ½ cup freshly grated parmesan cheese plus additional for garnish
 1½-2 pounds skinless, boneless chicken breasts
 3-4 tablespoons butter
 Flour seasoned with salt and pepper
 Cooked fettuccine or other pasta

1. Heat oil in 2-quart sauce pan, add bacon and Canadian bacon; cook over medium heat about 5 minutes. Add mushrooms, green onions and garlic; cook 3-4 minutes. Add tomatoes, olives and spices and cook another 3-4 minutes. Pour in wine and boil lightly about 5 minutes.
2. Reduce heat, sprinkle and stir in flour thoroughly. Gradually stir in heavy cream and half and half. Simmer until thickened. Stir in ½ cup parmesan; set aside. (Or refrigerate until ready to finish cooking.)
3. Remove all fat from chicken breasts and flatten them with heel of hand. Heat some of the butter in large frying pan. Toss breasts in seasoned flour; shake off excess. Brown and cook chicken, about 3-4 minutes per side. It may be necessary to keep some of the breasts warm while you cook the rest, using more butter if necessary.
4. Return all chicken to pan, pour in sauce; heat through. Serve over fettuccine noodles and garnish with additional parmesan cheese.

Chicken Provençale
Serves 4-6

The best tasting sauces needn't always contain cream and butter. The savory components of Provençale sauce include tomatoes, mushrooms, green pepper, ripe olives, dry white wine, garlic and olive oil. Not only is it low in cholesterol, it has both vibrant flavor and gorgeous color. Like so many of our sauté dishes, Chicken Provençale is easily managed in rushed restaurants or busy home kitchens; the easy-method sauce is made ahead of time and the chicken breasts are sautéed quickly at the last minute.

A steamed green vegetable plus rice pilaf, fettuccine or couscous are particularly fine with this dish. For a healthy vegetarian version, skip the chicken altogether.

Sauce Ingredients:
>   2 tablespoons olive oil
>   1½ cups sliced mushrooms
>   1 cup chopped green pepper
>   1 bunch green onions, chopped
>   1 cup sliced black olives (reserve the brine)
>   1 teaspoon minced garlic
>   1 can (10-14 ounces) crushed tomatoes or tomato puree
>   2 cans (each 6 ounces) tomato paste
>   1 cup dry white wine
>   1 cup olive brine
>   2 teaspoons dried basil
>   ½ teaspoon salt
>   ½ teaspoon ground black pepper

Sauté Ingredients:
>   4 tablespoons butter, clarified butter or olive oil
>   6 boneless, skinless chicken breasts (about 6 ounces each)
>   Flour seasoned with salt and pepper

>   Rice pilaf (or other starch)
>   Fresh sprigs of parsley or basil

1. To make sauce: Heat 2 tablespoons olive oil in sauce pan; add mushrooms, green pepper, green onion, olives and garlic. Cook 5 minutes. Add remaining sauce ingredients; simmer 45-60 minutes.
2. To sauté: Melt butter or olive oil in one or two large frying pans over medium high heat. Flatten chicken breasts with heel of hand, dredge in seasoned flour; shake off excess. Do not crowd chicken when you add it to the pan. Brown 3-4 minutes on the first side, turn and finish cooking another 3-4 minutes. Pour sauce over chicken; it may be held warm for a short time, but don't let chicken overcook. Serve over rice pilaf or other starch, and garnish with parsley or basil sprigs.

Chicken Marsala

Serves 4

Minced shallots acquire a mellow sweetness as they sauté with mushrooms, walnuts, and fresh parsley; blended with a Marsala wine glaze, these ingredients highlight fork-tender chicken breasts. Chicken Marsala is festive enough for company and quick enough for the end of a long day at the office. Boiled baby red potatoes or spinach fettucine, along with a garden fresh salad, complete the picture of a sophisticated but manageable meal.

If you find yourself without one of the listed ingredients, rest assured you can get equally successful results with pecans instead of walnuts, button mushrooms instead of shiitake, an onion/garlic combination instead of shallots, or another fortified wine (like port or sherry) instead of Marsala. Feel free to use this recipe as a jumping-off point for all kinds of inventive variations on the "sautéed chicken breast" theme.

4-6 boneless, skinless chicken breasts (about 6 ounces each)
Flour seasoned with salt and pepper
3-4 tablespoons butter or clarified butter
¼ cup minced shallots
2 cups sliced shiitake or button mushrooms
¼ cup chopped walnuts
1½ tablespoons chopped fresh parsley
½ cup Marsala wine
½ cup chicken stock
1-2 tablespoons additional butter (optional)
Salt and ground black pepper

1. Trim chicken breasts of all fat; flatten each with heel of hand, dredge in seasoned flour and shake off excess.
2. Melt butter in one or two large sauté pans over medium high heat. Do not crowd pan as you add chicken.
3. Lightly brown 3-4 minutes on the first side, turn and cook until almost tender, another 2 minutes or so.
4. Add shallots, then mushrooms and continue to cook another 2 minutes or so until mushrooms begin to get tender. Remove chicken breasts to a warm place. Add walnuts and parsley to pan.
5. Raise heat to high, add wine and chicken stock and boil until liquid reduces to a syrupy glaze. (If desired, you may swirl in additional butter at this point to enrich and bind the sauce.) Season to taste with salt and pepper.
6. Pour sauce over chicken; serve.

Brian's Chicken Tejano
Serves 4

Chicken with a southwestern accent and a no-stress method. Butter adds rich flavor but for a heart-healthy alternative use vegetable or olive oil.

Sauce Ingredients:
   1½ tablespoons butter or oil
   1 cup finely chopped onion
   ½ cup finely chopped celery
   ½ cup finely chopped green peppers
   1 small jalapeno pepper, minced
   2 teaspoons minced garlic
   1 cup chopped tomatoes, fresh or canned
   2 teaspoons each ground chili powder, ground cumin
      and dried coriander
   1 teaspoon garlic powder
   1 bay leaf
   ½ cup chicken stock or chicken bouillon dissolved in water
   ⅔ cup beer
   1 tablespoon lemon juice
   1 tablespoon cornstarch
   1 cup sour cream or sour half-and-half
Other Ingredients:
   1½ pounds boneless, skinless chicken breasts
   2 tablespoons butter or oil
   Flour seasoned with salt and pepper
   Cooked rice
   Chopped fresh coriander (optional)

1. To make sauce, melt 1½ tablespoons butter or oil in saucepan and sauté onion, celery, sweet and hot peppers until they soften. Add garlic and cook a few more minutes. Add tomatoes and spices; cook 5 minutes. Add chicken stock, beer and lemon juice; bring to simmer. Dissolve cornstarch in 1 tablespoon water and stir into sauce to thicken. Simmer 10 minutes; stir in sour cream. Set aside until ready to cook chicken.
2. To prepare chicken, remove all fat and flatten breasts with heel of hand. Heat 2 tablespoons butter or oil in large pan. Dredge chicken in seasoned flour and brown on first side 3-4 minutes; turn and continue cooking another 3-4 minutes. Add sauce; simmer until heated through. Serve over rice and sprinkle with fresh coriander, if desired.

Chicken Veronique

Serves 2-4

Here's an elegant entree that is very simple to prepare and quite different—tender chicken breast sautéed with grapes and glazed with a wine reduction sauce. You may use green, red or purple grapes and your favorite dinner wine. Chicken Veronique makes a lovely Valentine's meal, especially if you use red seedless grapes and a white Zinfandel . . . the finishing glaze will have a romantically rosy hue.

Serve the chicken breasts with a fresh green vegetable, rice pilaf and a glass of the same good wine used in the sauce.

> **4 skinless, boneless chicken breasts, each about 6 ounces**
> **Flour seasoned with salt and pepper**
> **2-3 tablespoons butter or clarified butter**
> **1 cup halved seedless grapes**
> **⅔ cup dry white or blush wine**

Flatten each chicken breast with heel of hand; dredge in seasoned flour, shaking off excess. Heat butter in large skillet and add chicken; do not crowd pan. (Do chicken in two batches, if necessary, keeping first batch warm while you do the second.) Cook on first side over medium heat for about 4 minutes, then turn and cook second side until just tender, about 3-4 more minutes. Do not overcook. Remove breasts and keep warm. Raise heat; add grapes and wine, scraping up any bits of flour or chicken that remain in pan. Simmer hard, stirring, until sauce is reduced to a light glaze. Ladle grapes and sauce over chicken; serve.

Chicken Cordon Bleu

Serves 4-6

Boneless breast of chicken is dressed with layers of ham and swiss cheese and draped with a gourmet mushroom sauce. Presented on rice pilaf, with a tender green vegetable like asparagus or snap beans, it makes a very classy meal.

4 tablespoons butter
6 boneless, skinless chicken breasts (about 6 ounces each)
Flour seasoned with salt and pepper
6 thin slices ham
6 slices swiss cheese
Cooked rice, rice pilaf or wild rice
Mushroom Sauce (page 84)

Melt butter in one or two large frying pans over medium high heat. Flatten chicken breasts with heel of hand, dredge in seasoned flour and shake off excess. Do not crowd chicken as you add it to the pan. Lightly brown 3-4 minutes on the first side, turn and cook until just tender, another 4 minutes or so. Place slice of ham and cheese on each breast, cover pans and cook over low heat until cheese is melted. Serve on white rice, rice pilaf or wild rice and blanket each serving with mushroom sauce.

"God sends meat, but the Devil sends cooks."
—Thomas Deloney

Southwestern Turnover

Makes 8 turnovers

Cuisines from all over the world have their own version of a savory stuffed pastry. Italian calzones, Polish pirogies, South American empanadas, and Cornish pasties are only a few. The doughs and fillings differ with the location; some are baked, some boiled, some deep-fried. We've tried many variations on Ovens menus through the years and have found all robust and delicious.

This turnover was developed at the Ovens of Brittany—Camelot Square when we introduced southwestern cooking to our menu. The recipe calls for puff pastry and an hispanic sausage called chorizo. The chorizo is combined with chicken and spicy salsa then baked inside the pastry with monterey jack cheese. We served it with rice pilaf, fresh fruit and extra salsa on the side (for those who like it hot). We were pleased with the results but even happier when this Southwestern Turnover won a prize in a national contest.

Look for chorizo in specialty delis or meat markets. (In Madison go to La Mexicana, a small grocery where you'll find three or four brands of the sausage

(continued on page 44)

Continued from page 43

and many other Mexican culinary staples). If you can't find chorizo, substitute hot Italian sausage. Hamburger just won't do.

Filling Ingredients:
¾ **pound boneless skinless chicken breasts**
½ **pound chorizo or hot Italian sausage**
1 **cup Tomato Salsa, recipe follows,** *OR* **use bottled salsa**

Other Ingredients:
1 **box (17¼ ounces) frozen, pre-rolled, ready-to-use puff pastry sheets (two sheets)**
Flour
Egg white
2 **cups grated monterey jack cheese**
Additional Tomato Salsa

1. To make filling, cut chicken into very small pieces. Heat skillet, add chorizo and break it up with a fork as it cooks. When sausage is crumbly add chicken and continue cooking until chicken is just tender. Drain well. Add salsa and chill thoroughly.
2. If you plan to cook turnovers right after they are assembled, preheat oven to 350 degrees. Grease a cookie sheet. (Or you may assemble turnovers, refrigerate and bake later.) Carefully thaw puff pastry according to package instructions. Keep dough cold after it has thawed by returning it to the refrigerator until you are ready to assemble turnovers.
3. On a floured surface, roll dough into two 14-inch by 9-inch sheets, and cut each into four 7-inch by 4½-inch rectangles. Brush entire dough surface with egg white.
4. Place ½ cup chicken/chorizo filling and ¼ cup grated monterey jack on bottom half of each rectangle. Fold top half over and press firmly along edges to seal the turnover. Trim the edges. Make one or two tiny slashes in the top of each turnover.
5. Place on baking sheet; bake 20-30 minutes until pastry is fully puffed and golden brown. Serve immediately, with additional salsa.

Variations: Make a Southwestern omelette by stuffing it with heated chicken/chorizo filling and cheese, and topping it with additional salsa. Yum. Or melt monterey jack cheese over the filling in the microwave, top with guacamole and chopped green onions. Serve this as a dynamite dip for tortilla chips.

Tomato Salsa

Makes 2½ cups

We know you like a fiery salsa for your nachos and burritos but there are dozens of ways to use this versatile condiment. Spike up a bowl of bean soup or tonight's broiled steak. Make a deviled egg even more fiendish or top the sour cream that tops your baked potato. Soy sauce and salsa combined make an arousing marinade for grilled chicken breasts. In potato salads, on side vegetables and in egg dishes of all kinds, salsa adds the kick we crave. Let your imagination go!

There are acceptable bottled salsas on the market today but why not make a spicy batch of your own? It's easy, inexpensive and since this recipe calls for canned tomatoes you can make it any time of the year. Of course, if you have a freezer full of last August's surplus, please go ahead and substitute your own tomatoes. Vary the "heat" according to your own tastes by adding more or less jalapeno and cayenne.

> 2 tablespoons vegetable oil
> 1 cup chopped onion
> 2 teaspoons minced garlic
> 1 jalapeno pepper, coarsely chopped
> 2 cans (each 16 ounces) whole peeled tomatoes, with juice
> 2 teaspoons cumin
> 2 teaspoons oregano
> 1 teaspoon dried coriander (optional)
> ½ teaspoon ground red (cayenne) pepper
> 1 teaspoon ground black pepper
> 1 teaspoon salt

Heat oil in saucepan. Add onion; cook over medium heat until onions are translucent. Add garlic and jalapeno; cook a few minutes longer. Coarsely chop tomatoes; add with can juices to onions. Stir in remaining ingredients; bring to simmer and cook about 45 minutes or until salsa is thick. Puree in food processor or blender (or puree only half and recombine with the unprocessed salsa for chunkier results). Can be served hot or cold.

Ovens Meatloaf

4-6 servings

When the Ovens of Brittany opened its first elegant dining room in downtown Madison, meatloaf as a menu item would have been unthinkable. Pâté, yes, but meatloaf, never! But in fact, pâté is just that . . . very fancy meatloaf. When the American taste for hearty home cooking finally became "fashionable," the Ovens was right there with a version of meatloaf to be proud of.

Jack Pollack, an Ovens chef for over 10 years, served this combination of ground beef and pork sausage flavored with onion, sweet pepper and herbs. Use a high quality bacon to top the loaf for it bastes the meat and adds a smoky flavor. A little Mushroom Sauce (page 84) ladled over the meatloaf slices dresses it up, but it's awfully good just plain, too.

    1 pound ground beef or ground chuck
    1 pound ground pork sausage
    ¼ cup minced green pepper
    ¼ cup minced onion
    2 eggs
    ¼ cup bread crumbs
    1 tablespoon dried parsley flakes
    1 tablespoon dried basil
    1 teaspoon salt
    ½ teaspoon ground black pepper
    4-6 strips of bacon

Preheat oven to 350 degrees. Combine all ingredients except bacon lightly but thoroughly (do not overmix the meat or it will toughen). Form into an oblong loaf and place in a baking dish. Lay bacon strips across the top and bake 1 hour and 15 minutes. Let rest 10 minutes before serving.

Tournedos Henri

Serves 4

Gone are the days when we consume oversized slabs of steak, but a modestly sized filet mignon is still very much a welcome sight. Wrapped in bacon, topped with sautéed artichoke hearts, and gilded with a tangy bearnaise sauce, Tournedos Henri (pronounced toor-neh-dohz ahn-ree) is an entree to keep in mind when you want to pull out all the stops without spending a week in the kitchen. Go-withs? Try Rissarole Potatoes (Page 68), fresh broccoli spears, and a bottle of husky red wine.

> **4 center cut beef tenderloin steaks, each 5-6 ounces**
> **4 slices bacon**
> **3 tablespoons clarified butter (see Terms and Techniques)**
> **4 whole canned artichoke hearts, well drained**
> **1 recipe Bearnaise Sauce (see below)**

1. Wrap each steak horizontally with a slice of bacon; secure with toothpicks.
2. Heat butter over medium high heat in heavy sauté pan just large enough to fit steaks without crowding them. Brown on first side for two or three minutes, then turn and brown other side. Lower heat and cook to desired doneness. Medium rare will take about 8-10 minutes. Halve the artichoke hearts. During the final minute or two of cooking, add the artichokes; brown lightly and heat through.
3. To serve, remove toothpicks, leaving bacon on the meat, and place steaks on individual plates. Place artichokes, cut side down, on meat, and spoon bearnaise on top.

Bearnaise Sauce

Makes 1 cup

Bearnaise, like hollandaise, is a dreamily rich butter sauce, but its piquant flavor comes from tarragon and vinegar instead of lemon juice. To make Bearnaise Sauce, use the recipe for Hollandaise on page 82, but substitute the following mixture for the lemon juice in that recipe.

> **3 tablespoons tarragon vinegar or white wine vinegar**
> **2 tablespoons dry white wine**
> **1½ teaspoons dried tarragon flakes**
> **1 tablespoon minced fresh shallots**

Combine all ingredients in a small saucepan; bring to a boil and reduce to one quarter of the original amount. Strain and cool the liquid. Proceed with Hollandaise recipe (page 82), substituting the vinegar reduction for the lemon juice.

Marinated Sirloin or Tenderloin Strips
Serves 4-6

A very easy Tex-Mex preparation, the lean meat is marinated and broiled whole, then thin-sliced for a restaurant-style presentation. Serve, if desired, with rice, corn tortillas, sour cream and salsa.

> **1 ½ pounds whole tenderloin or boneless sirloin steak**
> **1 small onion**
> **2 medium cloves garlic**
> **¼ cup olive oil**
> **Juice of one lime**
> **1 jalapeno pepper, seeded**
> **1 ½ tablespoons chili powder**
> **2 teaspoons ground cumin**
> **2 teaspoons oregano**

To make marinade: puree all ingredients except meat in food processor or blender. Place meat in glass dish just large enough to hold it; spread with marinade. Refrigerate several hours, turning often. Bring meat to room temperature; heat and oil broiler. Remove excess marinade from meat. Broil meat according to thickness and desired degree of doneness (5-9 minutes per side for medium rare). Let meat stand 3 minutes; slice thinly against the grain into strips.

"The nearer the bone, the sweeter the meat."
—Anonymous English proverb

Belgian Beef Carbonnade
Serves 6-8

Get ready for the heady aroma which will fill the room as you prepare this hearty peasant stew that partners beef, beer and onions. An initial searing of the meat in hot oil or bacon fat and a long, slow simmering process ensures achingly-tender meat. Dark beer and carmelized onions provide robust color and richness, while just a little brown sugar and vinegar produce a sweet-and-sour accent. Buttered noodles tossed with poppy seeds will help soak up every drop of this deeply delicious Belgian Beef Carbonnade. With brussels sprouts and plenty of cold, dark beer, it's the perfect antidote to winter's bluster.

> 3 pounds beef stew meat, cubed
> 4-6 tablespoons vegetable oil or bacon fat
> 6 cups thickly sliced onions
> 1 tablespoon minced garlic
> 1 cup beef or chicken stock
> 1 bottle (12 ounces) dark beer
> 1 teaspoon ground black pepper
> ¼ cup brown sugar
> 2 tablespoons dried parsley
> 1 tablespoon dried thyme
> 2 bay leaves
> 2½ tablespoons cornstarch
> 3 tablespoons red wine vinegar
> Salt and additional pepper

1. Preheat oven to 300 degrees. Heat a little oil or bacon fat until very hot in heavy frying pan. Brown beef in batches over high heat, taking care not to crowd the pan and removing browned pieces to a Dutch oven or other heavy, lidded casserole dish. Add more oil as you cook if required.
2. When all the meat is browned, reduce heat to moderate, and add a little more oil if necessary. Add onions; cook about 15 minutes, stirring often, until onions are golden brown and tender. Stir in garlic; cook 2-3 minutes longer, then add onion/garlic mixture to pot with beef.
3. Pour stock into frying pan, bring to boil and scrape up any bits stuck to bottom of pan. Pour this, along with the beer, pepper, sugar, parsley, thyme and bay leaves over the beef/onion mixture. Stir and bring to a boil on top of the stove. Turn off heat, cover pot tightly and bake in oven until meat is very tender, 1-2 hours.
4. Remove casserole from oven and skim fat from the surface. Return to simmer on top of stove. Combine cornstarch and vinegar; stir into simmering stew to thicken. Season to taste with salt and pepper. Can be served immediately, but tastes best the second day.

Cornish Pasty

Serves 6 big eaters

Many of the best dishes on Ovens menus have a rich European heritage, but none have a more curious and delightful past than the Cornish Pasty (pronounced pass-tee). Served at the Ovens of Brittany restaurant of the Chesterfield Inn in the historic mining town of Mineral Point, Wisconsin, the Cornish Pasty is a tasty reminder of that area's British heritage. How and why did the Cornish Pasty cross the ocean to become such a favorite in a small Midwestern town?

Like most of the world's best loved foods, pasties were originally a poor man's meal. They were created in Cornwall, England, where the mineral-rich hills made mining an arduous way of life. The miners' wives tucked hearty turnovers into their husbands' bib overalls for their mid-day meals. Toiling for long hours in the dark, dangerous tunnels, the rugged men relished the delicious and nourishing meat pies, still warm in their wrappings.

Today's pasties usually contain beef, potatoes, onions, and sometimes turnips or rutabagas, but in England anything was fair game in a pasty. It was said, in fact, that the Cornish must be good people, for the devil wouldn't dare cross the Tamar River into Cornwall, for fear that a clever Cornish woman would put *him* in a pasty!

It's also been said that "wherever you find a hole, you find a Cornishman," for they shared their famous mining skills the world over, settling wherever glaciers had left rich strains of lead and other minerals in mountains and hillsides. In the 1820's lead ore was discovered near the surface of a hill in what is now called Mineral Point, Wisconsin. It was the Cornish who came a few years later and showed the digging "Badgers" their more sophisticated means of removing precious minerals from deep inside the hills. The Cornish practice of cutting intricate tunnels to get to the long, rich veins of lead and zinc continued for over a century.

Today, the mines of Mineral Point are closed but Cornish customs like the avid consumption of pasties live on through the descendents of those early immigrants. Cornish specialities are served at the Ovens of Brittany of Mineral Point, which is housed in a quaint bed-and-breakfast establishment called the Chesterfield Inn. There, chefs follow instructions from two local women, Lela Jacobson and Evelyn Masbruch, whose recipes have been handed down for generations, and who make the best pasties this side of the Tamar River.

Pasties are plain, hearty food and in Mineral Point they are traditionally served with coleslaw, beet pickles and a sweet/sour chili sauce (a recipe is included here, but bottled chili sauce is acceptable). Turnip or rutabaga in the filling adds an authentic flavor, but is optional for those not so inclined. You can purchase lard from the refrigerated shelves at your grocer's and ask the butcher for suet, which is ground beef fat (you'll probably get it free of charge). Our recipe yields 6 very large pasties or twice that number if the pasties are made smaller. Leftovers freeze very well for later meals.

Crust Ingredients:
- 3 cups flour
- 1 teaspoon salt
- 1 cup (8 ounces) chilled lard, cut into small pieces
- 1 egg
- Ice water

Other Ingredients:
- 1½ pounds cubed sirloin tip or round steak
- 4 cups thinly sliced potatoes
- 1 cup diced turnip or rutabaga (optional)
- ½ cup chopped onion
- 3 tablespoons ground suet
- 1 tablespoon salt
- 1 teaspoon ground black pepper
- 3 tablespoons butter
- Flour

1. To make crust, mix 3 cups flour and salt. Cut in lard until size of small peas. Break egg into measuring cup; mix lightly. Add enough ice water to measure 1 cup. Add egg mixture to flour, tossing lightly with a fork until dough forms. Wrap in plastic wrap or wax paper; chill at least one hour.
2. To make filling, mix all remaining ingredients except butter and flour.
3. To form and bake pasties: Preheat oven to 400 degrees. Grease 1 or 2 large baking pans. On a floured surface, divide dough into six equal portions. Roll out each portion into an eight-or nine-inch circle. Divide filling into six portions and place each portion on bottom half of each dough circle. Place ½ tablespoon of butter on each filling portion. Using extra flour to prevent sticking, fold dough over filling. Press to seal by folding small sections of dough to make a rope-like edge. Place on baking pans. Bake 15 minutes; reduce heat to 375 degrees; bake additional 30-35 minutes. Serve with bottled or homemade chili sauce (recipe follows).

Lela Jacobson's Chili Sauce

Makes 2½-3 cups

1 can (28 ounces) peeled tomatoes plus ½ cup "V8" vegetable juice,
    OR 4 cups peeled, seeded fresh tomatoes
½ cup finely chopped onion
½ cup finely chopped celery
½ cup finely chopped sweet bell pepper (red or green)
½ cup apple cider vinegar
¼ cup sugar
2 tablespoons brown sugar
1 teaspoon salt
½ teaspoon celery seed (whole)
½ teaspoon mustard seed (whole)
½ teaspoon whole cloves
1-inch piece cinnamon stick

1. If using canned tomatoes, chop fine and combine with can juices and the vegetable juice in a heavy saucepan. If using fresh tomatoes, chop fine and measure into heavy saucepan.
2. Add onion, celery and sweet pepper; bring to hard simmer and cook, stirring often, until concentrated, about 30 minutes.
3. Add vinegar, sugars, salt, celery seed and mustard seed. Tie cloves and cinnamon in cheesecloth or place in tea infuser; add to sauce. Return to simmer; reduce again until thick, about 1 hour. Remove spice bag. Serve hot or cold.

Note: At home, Mrs. Jacobson makes five quarts of her Chili Sauce at a time (and at the Ovens of Britany in Mineral Point, the amounts would stagger the mind!). She cans the cooked sauce in pints, processing them for 10 minutes in a boiling water bath. You may want to consider making a large batch and sharing some with friends, for Lela Jacobson's Chili Sauce is great with eggs, chicken and beef of all cuts.

"There's no sauce in the world like hunger."
—Miguel de Cervantes, *Don Quixote,* 1605-1615

Ovens of Brittany

FISH & SHELLFISH

Seafood Sauce for Crêpes or Pasta
Serves 4

This scrumptious sauce originated from *Paul Prudhomme's Louisiana Kitchen*, the book that made Blackened Redfish famous. We took some of the Cajun heat out of the sauce, in response to pleas by a few teary-eyed customers. Our calmer combination of shrimp, crab and clams in a richly herbed sauce is fantastic on pasta or in crêpes.

>   **3 tablespoons butter**
>   **¼ cup minced yellow onion**
>   **1 cup heavy cream**
>   **Clam juice or fish stock: for crepes, use ¼ cup,**
>   **for pasta sauce, use 1 cup**
>   **½ teaspoon basil**
>   **¼ teaspoon oregano**
>   **¼ teaspoon thyme**
>   **¼ teaspoon salt**
>   **¼ teaspoon ground white pepper**
>   **½ cup chopped green onion**
>   **1½ tablespoons flour**
>   **⅔ pound shrimp, peeled and deveined**
>   **½ pound crabmeat, shredded**
>   **⅓ pound chopped fresh or canned clams**
>   **Cooked linguini or crêpes (page 73)**

1. Melt butter in heavy saucepan, add yellow onion and cook until translucent. Meanwhile, heat cream and clam juice together.
2. Add spices one at a time to the onion, stirring after each addition. Mix in green onion and flour and cook over low heat, stirring for about 3 minutes.
3. Whisk in hot cream mixture and simmer a few more minutes.
4. Stir in seafood and return to simmer; cook gently a few minutes until seafood is just tender.
5. If you are serving this as a pasta sauce, serve immediately over hot linguini noodles. If you are using it as a crepe filling, it can be chilled until ready to use, then divide ¾ of it equally among eight crêpes. Place crêpes in a buttered baking dish and bake in an oven (preheated to 350 degrees) for about 20 minutes. Heat the remaining sauce and ladle it over the heated crêpes.

Cajun Shrimp Diane
Serves 4

Louisiana Chef Paul Prudhomme has inspired so many cooks that his influence seems to touch every corner of America. Though the Ovens was featuring Cajun specialties before hot-and-spicy was the fad, it was Chef Prud homme's book, *The Louisiana Kitchen*, which gave us our most memorable and long-lasting recipes. We've made a few changes to his Shrimp Diane but it retains its Cajun zing, so if you like it hot, this one is for you.

Seasoning Ingredients:
¾ teaspoon ground red (cayenne) pepper
½ teaspoon salt
½ teaspoon ground black pepper
½ teaspoon dried basil
½ teaspoon dried thyme
½ teaspoon dried oregano
½ teaspoon garlic powder
¼ teaspoon ground white pepper

Other Ingredients:
3 tablespoons butter
2 teaspoons minced garlic
1 pound medium-size shrimp, peeled and deveined
½ pound sliced mushrooms
½ cup seafood stock or bottled clam juice
½ cup chopped green onions
Additional butter (optional)
Cooked white rice or rice pilaf
Chopped fresh parsley for garnish
Lemon wedges for garnish

1. Combine seasoning ingredients in a small bowl.
2. Melt butter in large frying pan, add garlic and seasoning mix, and cook gently for a minute or two.
3. Add shrimp, raise heat to medium high and add mushrooms. Cook a few minutes until mushrooms are half done.
4. Add seafood stock or clam juice and cook over very high heat until liquid reduces by half, then toss in green onions. Do not overcook, or the shrimp will toughen. (If desired, you may enrich the sauce by swirling in additional butter at this point.)
5. Serve over hot white rice or rice pilaf and sprinkle with chopped fresh parsley. Garnish with lemon wedges. Beer is recommended as a cooling accompaniment.

Scallops Fettuccine
Serves 4

½ teaspoon garlic powder
½ teaspoon garlic salt
¼ teaspoon ground white pepper
½ cup clam juice
1 tablespoon flour
1 cup half-and-half
1 cup heavy cream
4 ounces (about 1 cup) freshly grated parmesan cheese
3 tablespoons lemon juice
Salt and additional ground white pepper to taste
¾ pound fettuccine pasta
2 tablespoons butter
1 pound fresh scallops

1. Mix garlic powder, garlic salt and white pepper in a heavy saucepan. Stir in clam juice; mix in flour thoroughly. Turn on heat to medium; cook until thickened, stirring often.
2. Whisk in half-and-half and cream. Heat thoroughly and slowly. Turn off heat and whisk in parmesan a little at a time until sauce is thick and smooth.
3. Add lemon juice and season to taste with salt and additional white pepper. Sauce can be held at this point until ready to serve.
4. Cook fettuccine in boiling salted water until just tender. Meanwhile, melt butter in large skillet and gently cook scallops a few minutes until just tender. Add sauce and simmer a minute or two longer. Drain pasta, mix well with the sauce and serve.

Scallop Sauté
(With Tomato, Garlic and Parsley)
Serves 2-4 (or 6 as appetizer)

No cholesterol and no fuss. For an entree, serve this dish with rice or toss with vermicelli noodles that have been coated with a little olive oil. Or serve alone as an appetizer.

4 tablespoons olive oil
1 pound bay scallops
Flour seasoned with salt and pepper
2 teaspoons minced garlic

1 cup chopped fresh tomato
2 tablespoons chopped fresh parsley
Salt and freshly ground black pepper

Heat oil over medium-high heat in large pan. Meanwhile, toss scallops in seasoned flour and shake off the excess. Add to pan and saute 2-3 minutes. Add garlic; toss and cook another 2 minutes. Add tomato and parsley and heat through. Cook only until scallops are just tender. Season with salt and pepper.

Shrimp With Apples and Snow Peas
Serves 2-4

Full credit for this alliance of shrimp, tart apples, snow peapods, mustard and cream goes to Julee Rosso and Sheila Lukins, authors of the celebrated *Silver Palate Cookbook*. To meet the needs of a hectic restaurant, we've simplified their cooking method, and have found our way works well in home kitchens, too. You can make the sauce ahead and finish the recipe later in a few short minutes. We especially like the comely colors of this dish . . . the pale pink of tender shrimp, garden-green snowpeas and a delicately yellow mustard sauce, all served on snowy-white rice.

3 tablespoons butter, divided
¼ cup minced shallots
½ cup dry white wine
3 tablespoons Dijon-style mustard
½ cup crème fraîche (page xiv) or heavy cream
1 pound shrimp, peeled and deveined
1½ cups peeled, chopped tart apple (don't use Red Delicious)
¼ pound snow peas, stringed
1 teaspoon sugar
Salt and ground white pepper
Cooked white rice

Melt 1 tablespoon of butter in saucepan; add shallots, cover and cook gently 10 minutes. Remove cover, add wine, increase heat and reduce to one third of original amount. Reduce heat, stir in mustard and crème fraîche or cream; simmer 20-30 minutes, stirring occasionally. Sauce can be cooled and refrigerated until ready to use. For final cooking, melt remaining 2 tablespoons butter over medium high heat in large pan. Add shrimp, apples, snow peas, and sugar. Toss and cook 6 minutes, until almost tender. Stir in sauce and simmer gently until heated through. Serve with rice.

Seafood in Tomato Brandy Cream Sauce
Serves 4-6

In this mouth-watering recipe, shrimp (or other succulent pleasures from the deep) collaborate with sweet bits of grated carrot and ripe tomato in a lemon-accented brandy cream sauce. Respectfully borrowed and modified from a now forgotten source, Seafood in Tomato Brandy Cream Sauce became one of the most requested pasta specials at the Ovens of Brittany—Camelot Square. Though usually served on pasta, it will also get rave reviews on rice, or in crêpes or patty shells.

3 tablespoons butter, divided
2 tablespoons flour
3 tablespoons olive oil
¼ cup minced onion
2 tablespoons grated carrot
1 bay leaf
1 tablespoon finely grated lemon peel
⅓ cup brandy
¾ cup bottled clam juice
1 cup chopped, peeled, fresh tomato
¾ cup heavy cream
¼ teaspoon ground black pepper
1½ pounds peeled, deveined shrimp or other seafood

1. Make a roux by melting 2 tablespoons butter in small saucepan. Stir in flour and mix well. Cook over low heat, stirring often, 3-5 minutes. Remove from heat; set aside.
2. Heat olive oil and remaining tablespoon of butter in heavy saucepan and sauté onion, carrot, bay leaf and grated lemon peel over low heat about 10 minutes.
3. Pour brandy over mixture and, if desired, set aflame. After flames die, add remaining ingredients except seafood; bring to a simmer.
4. Whisk in roux until liquid is smooth; simmer 10 minutes.
5. Add shrimp or other seafood; cook gently a few minutes until seafood is just tender. Season to taste with salt and more black pepper, if desired.

Shrimp Dijon

Serves 3-4

1 pound large shrimp, peeled and deveined
3 tablespoons butter or clarified butter
3 tablespoons minced shallots or onion
1 teaspoon dried thyme
½ cup dry vermouth
½ cup heavy cream
3-4 tablespoons Dijon-style mustard
Salt and ground white pepper
Cooked white rice
Green and red sweet pepper rings
Chopped green onion

Heat butter in large sauté pan over medium high heat. Add shrimp and shallots; toss and cook 1-2 minutes. Add thyme and vermouth; stir and reduce a minute or so. Stir in heavy cream and mustard; continue to cook until shrimp are just tender and sauce is reduced to desired consistency. Season with salt and white pepper. Serve on rice, garnished with sweet pepper rings and chopped green onion.

"Will you walk a litter faster? said a whiting to a snail.
There's a porpoise close behind us, and he's treading on my tail.
See how eagerly the lobsters and the turtles all advance!
They are waiting on the shingle—will you come and join the dance?
Will you, won't you, will you, won't you, will you join the dance?
Will you, won't you, will you, won't you, will you join the dance?"
—Lewis Caroll, *Alice's Adventures in Wonderland*

Poached Salmon Fillets
With Cucumber Dill Sauce
Serves 4

Sauce Ingredients:
> 2-3 medium cucumbers, peeled, seeded and chopped
>   (to make 2 cups chopped)
> 1 teaspoon dried dill weed OR 1 tablespoon chopped fresh dill
> ½ teaspoon minced garlic
> ¼ cup mayonnaise, sour cream, or yoghurt
> ¼ teaspoon salt
> ⅛ teaspoon ground black pepper
> 1/16 teaspoon ground red (cayenne) pepper

Poaching Ingredients:
> 4 fillets (each 6 ounces) fresh salmon
> Dill weed
> ½ lemon
> 1 cup dry white wine

1. To make sauce: puree all sauce ingredients in food processor or blender. Chill, if desired.
2. To poach fish: sprinkle fillets with dill weed. Squeeze lemon juice into a deep pan large enough to hold all the fillets. Add wine, lemon rind and enough water to bring level to about 3 inches.
3. Bring liquid to low simmer; add fillets and poach very gently about 7-8 minutes, until just done. Drain carefully. Chill fish. Serve with cucumber sauce ladled down the middle of fillets. (May also be served warm.)

Salmon With Dill Mustard Sauce

Very special, and so easy it doesn't even need a recipe. Simply brush salmon steaks or fillets with melted butter and broil them, then serve with Dill Mustard Sauce, page 64. You may also poach the fish as outlined for Poached Salmon with Cucumber Dill Sauce, above. Or spread the fillets with Dill Mustard Sauce, splash with white wine and bake at 350 degrees for 12-20 minutes, depending upon their thickness. Dill Mustard Sauce is equally delicious with all kinds of fish, so try it out on your favorite.

Friday Night Fish Fry
Serves 4-6

You've not experienced Wisconsin until you've experienced a Friday night fish fry. All over the state, in dive bars, fancy restaurants and family establishments, perch, cod, haddock (you name it) are dipped in batter, deep-fried until golden brown and served to hordes of tradition-hungry customers. With coleslaw, cold beer and "your choice of potato," or with a whole array of buffet choices, it's our own special version of "Thank God It's Friday!" And if you're a true Midwesterner, there's really nothing else you hunger for at the end of the week.

        2 packages (each 1 pound) frozen or fresh cod
        1 cup flour
        ½ teaspoon paprika
        ½ teaspoon dried parsley flakes
        ¼ teaspoon ground red (cayenne) pepper
        ¼ teaspoon ground black pepper
        ¼ teaspoon garlic powder
        ¼ teaspoon garlic salt
        ¼ cup buttermilk
        ¾ cup beer
        2 tablespoons lemon juice
        Oil for deep-frying
        Flour seasoned with salt and pepper
        Tartar sauce

If using frozen fish, partially thaw cod in packages, about 2 hours. Meanwhile, combine flour and seasonings in bowl. Combine buttermilk, beer and lemon juice in separate bowl, then stir into flour mixture. Let stand 2 hours while cod thaws. To deep-fry, heat 3 inches of oil to 375 degrees. Cut cod into small "blocks" or separate into fillets. Dip cod first in seasoned flour, then in batter. Add pieces one at a time to oil and do not crowd them. Fry 4-7 minutes, depending upon thickness of fish. Fillets and fully thawed chunks of fish will take less time than partially frozen chunks. Drain on paper towels and keep warm while you fry remaining fish. Serve with tartar sauce.

Note: Other types of fresh or frozen fish may, of course, be substituted for the cod. Try orange roughy, haddock, or for true Wisconsin authenticity, lake perch.

Gratin of Sole

Serves 4

About 4 tablespoons butter, divided
3 tablespoons minced shallots or green onions
4 cups sliced mushrooms
1-1½ pounds sole fillets
Salt and ground black pepper
3 tablespoons minced fresh parsley
4 tablespoons dry white wine
4 tablespoons breadcrumbs

1. Preheat oven to 450 degrees. Butter a large, shallow baking dish.
2. Melt 2 tablespoons butter in large sauté pan; add shallots and cook over low heat until almost tender. Raise heat, add mushrooms and cook 3-4 minutes.
3. Season sole with salt and pepper; line bottom of baking dish with fillets. Spread mushroom mixture over fish, then sprinkle on parsley and wine. Top with bread-crumbs and dot with remaining butter.
4. Bake 10-12 minutes, until sole is just tender and breadcrumbs are lightly browned.

Note: Ingredients may be divided into individual baking dishes for an entertaining touch. Serve Gratin of Sole with tiny tender peas or asparagus spears, and rice pilaf.

Stuffed Trout

Serves 2

2 whole, fresh rainbow trout (about 8-10 ounces each)
½ cup toasted sliced almonds
¼ cup breadcrumbs
1 tablespoon melted butter or margarine
1 tablespoon minced fresh parsley
1 teaspoon dried thyme
1 egg white
Grated peel and juice of ½ lemon
Salt and pepper to taste
¼ cup dry white wine
Additional butter (optional)

Preheat oven to 350 degrees. Grease a baking dish. Combine all ingredients except trout, wine and additional butter. Stuff fish with the filling; place in baking dish. Sprinkle with wine and dot with additional butter, if desired. Bake 25-30 minutes.

Ovens of Brittany

SANDWICHES,
SIDE DISHES &
VEGETARIAN CHOICES

Hot Vegetable Sandwich

This healthy open-face stack is mouth-wateringly attractive, with colorful layers of broccoli, mushrooms, tomatoes, and onions, all blanketed with creamy melted cheese. Dill mustard sauce lavished on the bread slices adds a tangy touch. Even carnivores go for this one.

> **Slices of fresh bread**
> **Dill Mustard Sauce (recipe follows)**
> **Thin red or white onion circles**
> **Broccoli Filling (page 79) or chopped, cooked broccoli**
> **Thinly sliced fresh mushrooms**
> **Tomato slices**
> **Sliced cheese (cheddar, monterey jack, swiss, etc.)**

Preheat oven to 350 degrees. For each serving, spread copious amounts of dill mustard sauce on 2 slices of bread. Cut one of the slices in half diagonally and lay the two halves on the outer edges of the second slice, mustard side up, points facing outward. Place on baking sheet and layer all the vegetables as thick and as high as you dare. Bake for 10-15 minutes, or until vegetables are thoroughly heated, then top with cheese slices and bake a few minutes longer to melt the cheese. Serve hot.

Dill Mustard Sauce

Makes 2 cups

This is easy, easy, easy and extremely versatile. It'll keep for weeks in your refrigerator. Spread Dill Mustard Sauce on sandwiches or scrambled eggs, or smear it on grilled fish. Add it to tuna salad or egg salad or thin it with oil and vinegar for a piquant salad dressing. It'll perk up your Fourth of July hot dog and add new interest to your Easter ham. The list goes on and on!

> **¾ cup Dijon-style mustard**
> **1 cup mayonnaise**
> **1½ teaspoons dried dill weed OR 1 tablespoon chopped fresh dill**
> **1-2 tablespoons lemon juice**

Mix all ingredients.

Turkey Divan Sandwich

Another appealing open-faced sandwich, this one made special by using croissants instead of bread. Be generous with the dill mustard and pile the turkey and broccoli high. The choice of cheese to melt over it all is yours, and if you want to do it the Ovens way, serve Mornay Sauce (page 83) on the side. Ham, chicken or smoked turkey make excellent substitutes for the roast turkey. Wedges of fruit make a refreshing accompaniment.

Croissants, split horizontally
Dill Mustard Sauce, (see preceding recipe)
Slices of roast turkey
Broccoli Filling (page 79) or chopped, cooked broccoli
Sliced cheese (cheddar, monterey jack, swiss, etc.)
Mornay Sauce (optional, page 83)

Heat oven to 350 degrees. Spread dill mustard sauce over cut surfaces of croissant halves. Place the two halves of each croissant together, rounded sides down, pointed ends slightly overlapping, on an ungreased baking sheet. Pile on turkey slices, then broccoli. Bake 15 minutes, then top with cheese and bake a few minutes more, until cheese is melted. If desired, serve with Mornay Sauce.

Baked Brie

Next time you get a guilty urge to throw a TV dinner in the oven or microwave, consider making this fantastic open face cheese sandwich instead. It takes about as much time to assemble Baked Brie as it does to open and tend a frozen entree, and it is infinitely more satisfying. Luscious in its simplicity, Baked Brie requires only fresh fruit to set it off perfectly. It also works beautifully as an appetizer or "side" bread.

French bread
Slices of brie cheese (leave rind on)
Toasted slivered almonds

Preheat oven to 450 degrees. Slice french bread diagonally one inch thick and place pieces on an ungreased baking sheet. Cover bread with slices of brie; sprinkle on slivered almonds and bake 5-8 minutes, until cheese is melted.
Serve hot.

Olive and Nut Sandwich Filling

2 servings

The story of our Olive and Nut Sandwich is just a little sad. The inspiration for this interesting sandwich came from a wonderful, landmark restaurant located in Green Bay, Wisconsin. Kaap's, known for its high-back, dark wood booths, sumptious homemade candies and pastries, and authentic German specialties, enjoyed almost legendary status in Green Bay. It wasn't unusual for the waitress to be a 20-year veteran of the restaurant or for her to take large orders sans paper and pencil. Unfortunately, Kaap's was torn down to make way for more shopping and a treasured tradition ended.

They say all good things must come to an end, and the Olive and Nut Sandwich is no longer on the Ovens' regular menu, either. But you can still enjoy a little of the past by making this simple blend of cream cheese, green olives and walnuts. Spread it on fresh bread and tuck in some thinly sliced cucumber and a few alfalfa sprouts. Try it also on crackers or in omelettes.

    1 package (8 ounces) cream cheese, softened
    ⅓ cup chopped walnuts
    ½ cup minced green olives
    ¼ teaspoon salt
    ⅛ teaspoon ground white pepper

Mix all ingredients.

Lemon Pilaf

Serves 4-6

    2 tablespoons butter
    ¼ cup minced onion
    ¼ cup minced carrots
    1 cup long-grain rice
    ½ teaspoon minced garlic
    2 cups chicken or vegetable stock
    ½ teaspoon finely grated lemon peel
    1 tablespoon fresh lemon juice
    Salt and ground white pepper to taste

Melt butter in saucepan. Add onions and carrots; cook until tender. Add rice, stir and cook until rice is lightly toasted. Add garlic; cook 1 minute more. Stir in stock, lemon peel and lemon juice. Bring to boil, reduce to simmer, cover tightly and cook over low heat about 15 minutes, until all liquid is gone. Remove from heat and let stand, covered, 5 minutes. Fluff with fork and season to taste with salt and white pepper.

Oven-Fried or Grilled Potatoes

Nothing complements an omelette better than a heap of crispy "home fries." Fried potato connoisseurs, however, can be a fussy lot. Does one slice or chunk the potatoes? Bake or grill them? Onions or no onions? Melted cheddar cheese or just good ol' catsup? Even the type of potato to be used is a worthy subject of debate. It's all up to you, of course. Here's some guidelines to help you decide.

Potatoes (red, waxy type or large "bakers")
Melted butter or a combination of butter and oil
Dried parsley flakes or other dried herbs
Salt and pepper
Sliced onions (optional)
Cheddar cheese slices (optional)

Cover the potatoes with plenty of cold water; bring to boil and cook until *just* tender . . . not a minute longer! This will take 15-20 minutes depending upon the age and size of the potatoes. Drain, rinse and cool overnight in refrigerator.

The following day, slice or chunk potatoes. To oven-fry, spread potatoes in single layer on greased baking sheets. Brush with melted butter (or butter/oil combination) and sprinkle with parsley, salt and pepper. Bake in preheated 450 degree oven until golden brown, tossing once or twice, about 10-20 minutes. Melt cheese over the top during last couple of minutes, if desired.

If you prefer to grill potatoes, melt butter/oil combination in heavy-bottomed pan. If desired, add onions and cook a few minutes, until they begin to get tender. Raise heat, add potatoes, herbs, salt and pepper. Do not turn them until a crust has formed on the bottom of potatoes. You may need to add more butter/oil when you turn them. Cook potatoes until brown and crispy. Again, melted cheese is optional.

Rissarole Potatoes

Serves 4-5

Here's a potato side dish that seems to attract as much attention as the main courses with which it is served. It's similar in name to Potatoes Rissolé, a French recipe that first simmers, then sautés, potatoes cut into the shape of tiny footballs. Rissarole Potatoes, as it has evolved at the Ovens, is much simpler to make and is, I think, far more interestingly seasoned. These chunky, buttery, savory potatoes are steam-roasted and are best served sizzling hot with broiled steak or panfried fish.

> 2 pounds potatoes (6-8 medium)
> 4 tablespoons butter
> ½ teaspoon paprika
> ½ teaspoon garlic salt
> ½ teaspoon celery salt
> ½ teaspoon onion salt
> ¼ teaspoon ground black pepper

Preheat oven to 450 degrees. Peel potatoes, cut into large chunks and place in a baking dish. Cut butter into small pieces and distribute over potatoes. Sprinkle spices evenly over all. Add water to come one quarter of the way up the potatoes. Do not cover. Bake 30 to 45 minutes, until tender. If any liquid remains, it can be strained into a sauce pan, reduced over high heat and drizzled back over the potatoes.

Honey Squash

Serves 4

For a glorified version of pureed squash, we add a bit of golden-flavored honey and a splash of spirits.

> 1 or 2 acorn squash (2½-3 pounds total)
> 1½ tablespoons honey
> 2 tablespoons butter
> 2-3 tablespoons Madeira, bourbon, or brandy
> Salt and pepper to taste

Preheat oven to 350 degrees. Halve the squash and remove seeds. Place face down on greased baking dish. Bake until tender, 1-1½ hours. Scrape out "meat" into mixing bowl. Add remaining ingredients. Whip with electric beaters until smooth. Serve hot.

Pasta California
Serves 2

A real treat for blue cheese lovers.

> 3 tablespoons butter, divided
> 1 small onion, thinly sliced (about ½ cup)
> ⅓ cup dry white wine
> ⅔ cup heavy cream
> ½ teaspoon tarragon flakes or dried basil
> 4 ounces blue cheese, crumbled (about 1 cup)
> Ground white pepper to taste
> ½ cup thinly sliced carrots
> 1 cup broccoli flowerettes
> ½ cup thinly sliced green or red sweet peppers
> ½ cup sliced mushrooms
> 6 ounces linguine or fettuccine, cooked, rinsed with cold water,
>   drained and tossed with a little olive oil
> 2 tablespoons fresh or frozen peas

1. Melt 1 tablespoon butter in small saucepan; add onion and cook slowly until translucent.
2. Add wine, cream, and tarragon or basil. When mixture is hot, sprinkle in blue cheese and stir over low heat until cheese is melted and sauce is smooth. Season with ground white pepper. Sauce will be thin. Remove from heat (can be refrigerated until ready to use).
3. Melt remaining 2 tablespoons butter in sauté pan; add carrots and broccoli and cook over medium high heat 2-3 minutes, then add peppers and mushrooms and cook, stirring often, another 2-3 minutes.
4. Reduce heat, add sauce and cooked pasta. Cook for a few moments at a low simmer, tossing pasta with vegetables and adding peas during the last minute. Serve when most of the sauce has been absorbed by the pasta, taking care not to overcook the vegetables.

Southern Fried Tomatoes

Serves 4-6

To give Southern Fried Tomatoes an Italian flavor, substitute olive oil for the butter and basil for the parsley.

3-4 tablespoons butter
4 medium tomatoes
Flour seasoned with salt and pepper
1 egg mixed with 2 tablespoons water
⅔ cup breadcrumbs mixed with 1 tablespoon dried parsley

Heat butter in large frying pan. Thickly slice the tomatoes. Dip each in seasoned flour, then in egg/water mixture, then in breadcrumbs. When butter is very hot, add tomatoes and cook until golden brown on first side, then turn and brown on other side. Serve immediately.

Ovens of Brittany Stir-Fry

Serves 2

After years of specializing in intricately prepared dishes made from natural ingredients like butter and cream, the Ovens of Brittany opened in Shorewood in 1981 with a new emphasis on lighter foods and healthier preparations. The design of the Shorewood kitchen included several huge woks built right into the stoves, and thus it was that stir-fries were introduced to Ovens customers. Adopting stir-fry cooking to the more traditionally designed kitchens of the other Ovens locations has been an on-going challenge. It has proved, however, that excellent stir-fries can be produced without a Chinese wok.

Wok or no wok, stir-fries should be in everyone's culinary repertoire, for they are loaded with nutrient-rich vegetables and are cooked quickly in a minimal amount of cholesterol-free oil. They are beautiful to behold, kind to the budget and invite variation. Stir-fries are good for you, good to you, and, best of all, they *taste* really good.

Note: The vegetables in this recipe may be varied at will, and if you are non-vegetarian, add chicken strips, shrimp or lean meats. To spice it up, sprinkle in dried pepper flakes.

Sauce Ingredients:
>¼ cup water, vegetable stock or chicken stock
>2 tablespoons soy sauce or tamari
>1 tablespoon orange juice
>½ tablespoon honey
>1 tablespoon dry sherry
>⅛ teaspoon ground ginger
>⅛ teaspoon garlic powder
>⅛ teaspoon ground cloves

Stir-Fry Ingredients:
>3 tablespoons peanut, vegetable, or canola oil
>½ cup thinly sliced carrots (cut diagonally)
>½ cup thinly sliced broccoli tops and stems
>½ cup thinly sliced cauliflower
>¼ cup thinly sliced celery (cut diagonally)
>1 teaspoon minced garlic
>1 teaspoon grated fresh ginger root
>½ cup sliced mushrooms
>½ cup each red and green sweet pepper strips
>½ cup stringed snow peas
>¼ cup chopped green onions
>¼ cup bean sprouts
>¼ cup sliced water chestnuts
>1 teaspoon cornstarch (optional)
>Cooked rice

1. Combine sauce ingredients thoroughly. Set aside.
2. Prepare all vegetables as outlined above.
3. Heat wok or large heavy frying pan. Raise heat to highest point and add oil. Add carrots, broccoli, cauliflower and celery; toss lightly for about 2 minutes.
4. Add garlic, ginger root, mushrooms, red and green peppers and peapods. Toss for about 2 minutes.
5. Add green onions, bean sprouts and water chestnuts and toss again for 2 minutes.
6. Add sauce; bring to a boil. If you wish to thicken the sauce, you may sprinkle in 1 teaspoon cornstarch. Or, reduce sauce over high heat. Take care you don't overcook the vegetables; they should be crisp-tender. Serve over rice.

Spinach Gâteau

Serves 6

The French word "gâteau" means cake, but this rich, round, layered gâteau is a savory main course, not a dessert. While over the years at the Ovens, many gâteau fillings have been created, in this version seasoned spinach and mushrooms are alternated with delicate crêpes and three cheeses, then baked and topped with a creamy mornay sauce. Served in wedges with fresh fruit, Spinach Gâteau makes an impressive lunch or an elegant centerpiece for a vegetarian dinner.

To display this dish at the table, bake it in a spring-form pan, which is a round, flat-bottomed pan with a ring that locks on to form the sides of the pan. (Spring-form pans are most often used for baking cheesecakes.) To serve, remove the pan's ring and place the gâteau on a large platter for a beautiful presentation. If you don't own a spring-form, use any round baking dish or cake pan that is at least two inches deep.

Filling Ingredients:
>   1 tablespoon butter
>   ½ cup chopped onion
>   1 large garlic clove, minced
>   3 cups sliced fresh mushrooms
>   1 ½ pounds fresh spinach, cleaned, de-stemmed, cooked briefly
>   and chopped OR 2 boxes (each 10 ounces) frozen
>   chopped spinach, thawed
>   4 ounces (1 ½-2 cups) grated monterey jack cheese
>   1 container (15 ounces) ricotta cheese
>   1 tablespoon dried parsley
>   1 tablespoon oregano
>   1 teaspoon salt
>   ¼ teaspoon ground white pepper
>   ¼ teaspoon nutmeg

Other Ingredients:
>   20 crêpes, 6 to 8 inches in diameter (recipe follows)
>   Freshly grated parmesan cheese
>   Mornay Sauce (page 83)

To make filling:

1. Melt butter in skillet. Add onion and cook slowly until translucent, then add garlic and cook 1 minute more. Raise heat, add mushrooms; cook about 5 minutes until mushrooms are just tender. If mushrooms start to give off moisture, raise heat higher to evaporate the water. Remove from heat and cool.
2. Meanwhile, drain spinach and squeeze out excess liquid. Place in bowl with remaining filling ingredients. Add cooled mushrooms; mix gently but thoroughly.
3. To assemble and bake: Grease a round baking dish (8 to 9 inches in diameter and at least two inches deep) or spring-form pan. Lay four over-lapping crêpes on bottom of pan and up sides a little. Press about one cup of filling evenly over crêpes. Repeat this process three more times, then top the last layer of filling with one more layer of crêpes. Gâteau may be chilled at this point until ready to bake.
4. To bake, preheat oven to 350 degrees; bake gâteau 40-50 minutes. Sprinkle freshly grated parmesan over the surface and continue to bake for about 5 minutes until cheese is melted. Cut gâteau into wedges; serve with hot mornay sauce.

Crêpes
Makes 20-24 crêpes

6 eggs
½ teaspoon salt
¼ teaspoon nutmeg
⅓ cup unbleached all purpose flour
¼ cup whole wheat flour *OR* use all white flour if desired
2 tablespoons vegetable oil
1 cup water
Vegetable oil for cooking

(continued on page 74)

Continued from page 73

Beat eggs, then add salt and nutmeg. Mix in white flour, then whole wheat flour. Add oil and water; stir until smooth. Batter should be thin and must be stirred often as you cook the crêpes one by one.

Heat a 7- or 8-inch non-stick skillet. Add a little oil and swirl around to coat the bottom. Discard the hot oil. Pour about 2 tablespoons batter into bottom of pan and immediately turn pan back and forth and around to coat bottom. You can patch any "holes" with a bit more batter. Cook over medium heat until edges of crêpe begin to curl a bit. With a rubber spatula, loosen crêpe and gently flip it over. Cook one or two seconds more then slide crêpe onto a place. Crêpes should *not* brown. Repeat this process until all batter is used. Stir batter often; if it gets too thick, add a little water and continue cooking. (*Note:* if you use two skillets you can cut the cooking time in half.)

Crêpes are delicate and will tear easily, so handle carefully. They may be refrigerated or frozen for later use with your favorite sweet or savory fillings and toppings.

Cossack Pie

Serves 6

Professional cooking is hard work, with hot, tense kitchen conditions and frequently grim hours. But if you love to cook it's also rewarding work, and it is the very best cooks who also make the job fun. Tim Lloyd, the creator of the following recipe, is a "case" in point. He's a grinning, red-headed Bohemian with a passion for food *and* fun. Churning out orders with happy abandon and bewildering finesse, Tim keeps the staff laughing with his running comedy routine.

In the recipe below, Tim bakes cauliflower, cheddar cheese and sour cream in a mashed potato crust and calls it Cossack Pie. Why that name?, I ask Tim. "Why not!" he booms. "It just came to me. I *like* the name. I like Cossacks!" Cossack Pie it is.

Crust Ingredients:
  2 pounds baking potatoes (about 5-6 medium)
  3 tablespoons sour half-and-half
  Salt and pepper to taste

SANDWICHES, SIDE DISHES & VEGETARIAN CHOICES

Filling Ingredients:
> 2 tablespoons butter
> ½ cup chopped onion
> 1 teaspoon minced garlic
> 4 cups chopped cauliflower
> 1 tablespoon dried basil or thyme
> 1 teaspoon salt
> ½ teaspoon ground white pepper
> ½ cup sour half-and-half (a lower fat sour cream)
> ¼ cup milk
> 1 egg
> 2 cups grated sharp cheddar cheese (about 8 ounces)
> Additional grated cheddar or parmesan cheese (optional)
> Paprika or chopped fresh parsley

1. To make crust, peel and boil potatoes in salted water until very tender. Mash potatoes with 3 tablespoons sour half-and-half; add salt and pepper to taste. Potatoes should be stiff but not lumpy.
2. Preheat broiler. Lightly press potatoes into a greased deep-dish pie or quiche pan. Build up the edges of the crust above the top of the pan. Broil 4-6 minutes until lightly browned and firm. Remove crust from oven and cool. Turn oven down to 350 degrees.
3. Make filling by cooking onions and garlic in butter for several minutes. Add cauliflower and basil or thyme; cover and cook until tender, about 10 minutes. Add salt and white pepper.
4. Make custard by combining ½ cup sour half-and-half, milk and egg.
5. Layer one cup cheddar cheese on bottom of crust. Spread cauliflower over it, then add remaining cheese. Pour custard over all and move the cauliflower around lightly to let custard reach bottom of pie.
6. Bake 40-45 minutes, until custard is set. You may melt additional cheese over the top for the last few minutes, if desired. Sprinkle with paprika or chopped fresh parsley and serve.

Note: This recipe invites substitutions and additions of your choice. Broccoli can be happily swapped for the cauliflower. For a smokey touch consider adding bacon bits or chopped ham. If you want to stick to the vegetarian theme, chopped green pepper or sliced mushrooms can be sautéed with the cauliflower.

Vegetarian Stroganoff
Serves 2

This recipe calls for crème fraîche, a thick, tart cream similar to sour cream. Though it's a snap to make, crème fraîche develops texture and flavor over time and must be prepared at least 2 days before use. Both crème fraîche and red wine give unusual character to this easy and very delicious Vegetarian Stroganoff.

2 tablespoons butter
½ cup chopped onion
1 cup sliced mushrooms
½ teaspoon minced garlic
½ cup dry red wine
¾ cup crème fraîche (page xiv)
1 large tomato, cut into eighths
¾ cup stringed snow peas
Salt and pepper to taste
Buttered noodles tossed with chopped fresh parsley

Heat butter in large sauté pan. Cook onions over medium heat until they begin to soften. Raise heat; add mushrooms and garlic and cook 2-3 minutes. Add wine; reduce for a minute. Add crème fraîche and reduce until thickened, about 4 minutes. Stir in tomato and snow peas and cook until vegetables are just tender, about 2 minutes more. Season to taste with salt and pepper. Serve with noodles.

Note: If you double this recipe, reduce the sauce for a longer period of time to obtain the desired thickness. Don't add the tomatoes and peapods until a minute or two before the sauce is done, or they will be overcooked.

"There are many ways to love a vegetable. The most sensible way is to love it well-treated. Then you can eat it with the comfortable knowledge that you will be a better man for it, in your spirit and your body too . . ."
—M.F.K. Fisher, *How to Cook a Wolf,* 1951

Ovens of Brittany

BREAKFAST &
BRUNCH CHOICES

The Simple Art of Making Omelettes

It doesn't take years of disciplined practice to master the art of cooking omelettes. It is actually one of the easiest and quickest dishes one can create. Why *is* there something a bit . . . mysterious about making omelettes? Kitchen trainees at the Ovens of Brittany stand in awe of seasoned breakfast chefs who turn out dozens of omelettes in a matter of minutes. But those green cooks soon become experts themselves. Omelettes are *fun* to make and grand to serve, and they fit into any meal of the day (or night)! If there is a little mystery surrounding them, I think it's because these omelettes are inexplicably delicious.

Here are the guidelines to enlighten your path in the art of making omelettes. Favorite recipes for fillings come next, and then a list of sauces and more filling ideas.

1. First, your equipment. About the only essential is a non-stick skillet with sloping sides, 6-8 inches in diameter. For heftiness, good heat distribution and durability, a good choice is Wearever brand with a Silverstone brand surface . If you don't have a non-stick pan, try a heavy pan in good condition and melt extra butter in it when you get to that point in the recipe. Also handy to have are a rubber spatula, a ladle and a whisk. Warmed serving plates add a professional touch.

2. Now, the eggs. Figure two or three fresh whole eggs per person. Crack them into a bowl and add a tablespoon of water for every three eggs. (You may also add any leftover egg whites you have from other recipes). Don't add salt or pepper; you can put that in the filling or let your guests season their own omelette. With a whisk or fork, whip the eggs.

3. Prepare or heat filling and sauce and keep them nearby. From here on in, things go *fast*.

4. To cook a single omelette: Heat pan over medium flame for a minute or two. Melt two teaspoons butter in pan; raise heat to high. When butter is frothy and sizzling (but not burned!) add a ladle of "egg juice" to the pan. (One half cup is about 2 large eggs worth; if you are making 3-egg omelettes, figure ⅔ to ¾ cup per omelette). The egg will immediately begin to set on bottom of pan. With a spatula or non-stick egg-lifter, pull the cooked egg from outer edges of pan towards center. The uncooked egg will spread and cook. Use the spatula to help spread liquid egg off the top of solidified egg and onto exposed sections of pan bottom. Continue to do this until nearly all the liquid egg is set. Reduce heat to very low. The egg will continue to cook as you spread filling across middle of omelette. (Flipping the omelette to finish its cooking adds flair to your performance but encourages one to overcook what should be a very tender product.)

French omelettes are moist inside and unbrowned or very lightly browned on the outside, though at this point you may cook it according to your preference. To serve the omelette, take the warmed plate in your left hand and grasp the pan handle with your right. (Vice versa if you are left-handed, of course). Hold the plate close to the pan. Shaking pan slightly, slip omelette onto plate, rolling omelette into either a "cigar" or "half-moon" shape by tilting one side of pan upwards and over filling. This entire step takes only a couple of minutes. You may hold cooked omelette briefly in a warm oven while you make the rest, then sauce and serve!

Broccoli Filling
(for Omelettes and More)
Makes about 3 cups

1 pound broccoli
1-2 tablespoons butter
½ cup chopped onion
1 cup sliced mushrooms
Salt and black pepper

Cut off broccoli stalks close to base of flowerettes. Peel stalks with sharp knife or potato peeler. Dice broccoli stalks and set aside. Chop flowerettes coarsely. Heat butter in skillet and cook broccoli stalk pieces with onions for about 5 minutes. Add mushrooms and broccoli flowerettes; cook another 5 minutes or until just tender. Season to taste with salt and pepper.

Cream Cheese and Herb Filling
Makes 1 cup

1 package (8 ounces) cream cheese, softened
1 ½ teaspoons freeze-dried chives *OR* 1 tablespoon fresh chives
½ teaspoon dried dill weed *OR* 1 teaspoon chopped fresh dill
¼ teaspoon celery salt
⅛ teaspoon ground white pepper

Combine all ingredients thoroughly. Use in omelettes or sandwiches or on crackers.

French Country Filling
Makes 4 cups

This is a ratatouille, the vegetable dish made from summer's bounty: eggplant, zucchini, sweet peppers, tomatoes, onions and Mediterranean herbs. Roll it into an omelette with grated Swiss cheese, and top with creamy Mornay Sauce (page 83). For double enjoyment, use French Country Filling as the sauce as well as the stuffing. It is equally delectable inside crêpes, empanadas, on rice or pasta, or all by itself.

   3 tablespoons olive oil
   ½ cup chopped onion
   ½ pound (about 1 ½ cups) unpeeled, diced eggplant
   ½ pound (about 2 cups) unpeeled, diced zucchini
   ½ cup diced green peppers
   1 cup chopped tomato (about 1 medium-sized)
   1 can (8 ounces) tomato sauce
   1 bay leaf
   1 teaspoon thyme
   1 teaspoon oregano
   1 teaspoon basil
   1 teaspoon salt
   1 teaspoon ground black pepper

Heat olive oil in skillet and cook onion over medium heat for several minutes, until tender. Add eggplant, zucchini, peppers and saute another 3-5 minutes. Stir in remaining ingredients and simmer 20-30 minutes. Taste and adjust seasoning.

"Good cooking does not depend on whether the dish is large or small, expensive or economical. If one has the art, then a piece of celery or salted cabbage can be made into a marvelous delicacy."
—Yuan Mei, *Poems* translated by Arthur Waley, 1956

Avocado Filling or Dip

Makes 1½ cups

2 ripe avocados
4 ounces cream cheese, softened
2 tablespoons fresh lemon juice
½ teaspoon cumin
¼ teaspoon ground red (cayenne) pepper

Peel and mash avocado. Combine with remaining ingredients. Use for filling omelettes, or as a refreshing dip for vegetables, or as a spread in sandwiches.

"As everybody knows, there is only one infallible recipe for the perfect omelette: your own."
—Elizabeth David, *French Provincial Cooking*, 1950

Omelette Recommendations

Sauces:

The tastiest and most versatile sauces to use as omelette toppings are **Mornay, Hollandaise, Tomato Salsa** and **Mushroom Sauce** (see Index for recipes). If time or resources are short, don't make a separate sauce, but accent your omelette with a little of whatever filling you are using.

Fillings:

Sautéed mushrooms and parmesan cheese
Fresh spinach, steamed, chopped and seasoned
Minced green olives in softened cream cheese
Ham or bacon or Canadian bacon bits
Leftover hot and spicy chili
Grilled potatoes and onions
Feta cheese and chopped Greek olives
Strawberry or raspberry preserves
Chicken/chorizo filling (page 44)
Chopped, cooked shrimp with fresh dill
Pesto
Chopped tomatoes, fresh herbs and grated mozzarella cheese
Roasted red, green, purple and yellow sweet peppers
Seafood Sauce for Crêpes or Pasta (page 54)

Hollandaise

Makes one cup

Hollandaise sauce is a luxury. You wouldn't want to have it every day, or even every week. Save it for special occasions, like Mother's Day or Easter brunch, or a visit to one of the Ovens of Brittany restaurants!

Making hollandaise *used* to be a very tricky, time-consuming business what with double boilers, heat adjustments and perpetual whisking. Food processors and blenders have changed all that. Read on.

> **3 large egg yolks**
> **Juice of ½ lemon**
> **½ pound melted butter, hot but not boiling**
> **Salt and ground red (cayenne) pepper to taste**
> **Small to medium capacity food processor OR**
> **blender with lid that has a removable center**

1. Have all ingredients ready and close at hand. Make sure food processor is clean and dry. Place yolks and lemon juice in processor bowl. Process until very well blended, about 1 minute.
2. With machine running, slowly add hot melted butter in a *thin* stream. After you get about half of the butter in, the sauce will begin to thicken and you'll begin to hear it "slap" against sides of bowl. At this point, you can add the butter a little faster. When all the butter is incorporated, turn machine off. Add salt and cayenne to taste and process a few seconds longer.
3. If sauce is too thick add a small amount of warm water and process a few seconds more. If sauce has not thickened, it's likely that your butter was not hot or that you added the butter too quickly. You can still save the day by pouring hollandaise into a heavy saucepan, placing it over a low flame, and whisk, whisk, whisk. It will thicken.

Note: If you have leftover hollandaise it will keep in the refrigerator for several days. To reheat, warm in the microwave 5 seconds at a time, stirring after each time. Or, heat over simmering water, stirring often.

Mornay Sauce

Makes about 2 cups

Mornay is an indispensable cheese sauce that can be made in a matter of minutes. Use it on omelettes and other egg dishes, and over fish, chicken or vegetables. Though we use a mixture of milk and heavy cream and two cheeses, you may substitute all milk and one cheese, if desired.

2½ tablespoons butter
3 tablespoons flour
1 cup milk
½ cup heavy cream
½ teaspoon salt
⅛ teaspoon ground white pepper
⅛ teaspoon nutmeg
2 dashes hot pepper sauce
¼ cup grated Swiss cheese
¼ cup freshly grated parmesan cheese

To make the roux, melt butter in saucepan and stir in flour until well blended. Cook over low heat, stirring often for 3-5 minutes. Meanwhile, gently heat remaining ingredients except cheeses in microwave or another pan. Whisk milk mixture into the roux until smooth. Simmer about 10 minutes, stirring often. Remove from heat and stir in cheeses, a little at a time, until well-blended and smooth. Thin with additional milk if desired. Taste and adjust seasoning.

"Cooking is a way of giving and making yourself desirable."
—Michel Bourdin q. in *Time* magazine, 1978

Mushroom Sauce

Makes 4 cups

Typical homecooked simplicities like baked potatoes, scrambled eggs and broiled chicken become something distinctive when adorned with the likes of this rich Mushroom Sauce. Since the recipe makes a lot of sauce, you can use it a number of different ways or freeze the leftovers for a quick but classy meal later on.

> **5 tablespoons butter, divided**
> **4 cups sliced mushrooms**
> **½ cup minced onions**
> **2½ cups milk**
> **2 tablespoons dried onion-mushroom soup mix**
> **¼ cup flour**
> **½ cup peeled, seeded, chopped tomatoes (fresh or canned)**
> **½ cup sour half-and-half (a lower fat sour cream)**
> **Dash or two of hot pepper sauce**
> **Salt and ground white pepper to taste**

1. Melt two tablespoons butter in sauté pan; add onions and mushrooms and cook over medium heat until tender. Set aside.
2. Heat milk and dried soup mix together in microwave or on stovetop.
3. Melt remaining 3 tablespoons butter in medium saucepan. Stir in flour. Cook over low heat, stirring often, for 3-5 minutes. Whisk in heated milk mixture until smooth and thickened.
4. Add mushroom mixture and tomatoes; simmer 10-15 minutes. Stir in sour half-and-half and season to taste with hot pepper sauce, salt and white pepper.

Potato Pancakes

Makes twelve 3-inch pancakes

If you own a food processor, you can make these delicious pancakes in a snap. But they are worth grating by hand, too. We like to substitute zucchini or carrot for some of the potato in the batter; this adds a sweeter flavor and bits of bright color to the finished product. Pair the pancakes with applesauce, maple syrup, or sour cream, then sit back and listen to the compliments.

¼ cup minced onion
2 eggs, lightly beaten
¼ cup flour
¼ cup yellow cornmeal
1 teaspoon salt
¼ teaspoon ground black pepper
1¼ pound (about 4 medium-sized) baking potatoes
Lemon juice (optional)
Vegetable oil
Applesauce, maple syrup or sour cream

1. Combine onion with eggs in small bowl. Mix flour, cornmeal, salt and pepper in a large bowl and set both bowls aside.
2. Scrub but do not peel potatoes. Grate them in a food processor or by hand. With a clean, dry towel, squeeze out as much liquid as possible from grated potatoes.
3. Combine potatoes and flour mixture, then use your hands to mix in egg and onion. You may add a little lemon juice to prevent the raw potato from turning brown.
4. Cover bottom of heavy skillet with ⅛ inch vegetable oil and heat oil until very hot. Add a ¼ cup scoop of batter to the hot oil and flatten quickly with a spatula or spoon. Continue with more scoops of mixture until pan is filled, but not crowded. Cook pancakes over medium-high heat until golden brown on both sides. Adjust heat if necessary to prevent oil from smoking. Drain cooked pancakes on paper towels.
5. Repeat this process until all the potato mixture is used up, adding more oil if required. Serve immediately with applesauce, maple syrup or sour cream.

Variation: Substitute ¼ cup grated zucchini or carrot for ¼ cup of the grated potato.

Cornmeal Whole Wheat Pancakes
Makes 10-12 pancakes (each 4 inches)

Light, healthy and easy-to-make, Cornmeal Whole Wheat Pancakes were first served at the Ovens of Brittany-Shorewood. When I tested them in my home kitchen, I couldn't resist sprinkling chocolate chips over the partially cooked pancakes in the pan. Maybe they weren't as healthy, but they were scrumtious!

1 egg
⅓ cup vegetable or canola oil
1 cup milk
½ cup whole wheat flour
½ cup yellow cornmeal
¼ teaspoon salt
2½ teaspoons baking powder
Oil for cooking

Whisk together egg, oil and milk. In a separate bowl, mix flour, cornmeal and salt. Add dry ingredients to the wet and mix lightly. Stir in baking powder. There may be a few lumps. Let rest 15-20 minutes. Lightly coat bottom of a non-stick skillet with oil and place over medium heat. When pan is hot, pour small amounts of batter into pan. Cook on one side until bubbles form over surface of pancakes. Flip pancakes carefully and cook until second side is done. Serve immediately.

"He who does not mind his belly will hardly mind anything else."
—Dr. Samuel Johnson

Rice Pudding

Serves 6

This is an old-fashioned dish that will warm and sooth you on a chilly morning. It's an inspired way to use up leftover cooked rice. You can make this homey dish more elegant by serving it the way we used to at the Ovens on Monroe. Cook the pudding in small, well-buttered ramekins and unmold them onto a plate. Heat chopped fresh fruit with a little honey and brandy, then arrange the fruit around the pudding and sprinkle a few toasted almond slivers over all.

> 3 eggs
> 1 cup heavy cream
> 1 teaspoon vanilla
> 1 teaspoon cinnamon
> 1/3 cup sugar
> 2/3 cup raisins
> 2½ cups cooked white rice, cooled

Preheat oven to 350 degrees. Mix eggs, cream, vanilla, and cinnamon, then combine with remaining ingredients. Bake in a greased baking dish for 35-40 minutes, or until just set.

"The proof of the pudding is in the eating."
—Henry Glapthorne, *The Hollander,* 1635

88

Bread Pudding With Apples
Serves 6-8

Surprise your guests by serving this wonderful Bread Pudding with Apples for brunch. It's a thrifty dish that transforms plain ingredients like apples, raisins and leftover bread into something rather grand. A goodly amount of whipped cream makes it positively sensuous; with sausage links, hot coffee and a medley of fresh fruit, you'll have a true feast.

Bread pudding also doubles as a dessert, especially if you serve it with Honey Rum Sauce, page 110. If you don't have individual baking dishes, you can use a larger single dish instead and bake it a bit longer.

 1 pound apples (about 3-4 medium)
 2 tablespoons butter
 1 tablespoon sugar
 3 eggs
 ⅓ cup brown sugar
 2½ cups milk
 ⅓ cup raisins
 1 teaspoon vanilla
 ½ teaspoon cinnamon
 ¼ teaspoon nutmeg
 ⅛ teaspoon salt
 8 cups cubed day-old french or raisin bread

1. Preheat oven to 350 degrees. Peel, core and cut apples into large chunks. Melt butter and sugar in a pan and sauté apples until soft. Set aside.
2. In a large bowl, combine eggs and brown sugar; mix in remaining ingredients except bread and apples.
3. Grease 6-8 individual (non-aluminum) baking dishes. Add bread and apples to egg/milk mixture and fill dishes. (Do not let the bread soak longer than a few minutes.) Wipe any drips from rim of dishes and place in a large baking pan. Add enough water to pan to reach one third way up dishes. Bake 30-40 minutes until set. Serve warm.

Apple Raisin Walnut Crêpes

Serves 6

2 packages (each 8 ounces) cream cheese, softened
2 cups chopped apples (about 2 medium apples)
½ cup raisins
½ cup chopped walnuts
3 tablespoons honey
½ teaspoon cinnamon
Pinch of nutmeg
12 crêpes (page 73)
Powdered sugar, whipped cream or jam

Preheat oven to 450 degrees. Grease a baking dish. Mix first 7 ingredients. Place 1-2 tablespoons of mixture along center of each crêpe and roll up. (Can be wrapped in wax paper until ready to bake.) Place in baking dish; bake 10 minutes. Serve with powdered sugar, whipped cream or jam. Serve two per person.

Oat Bran Granola

Makes about 1 quart

3½ cups oats
½ cup oat bran
½ cup sliced almonds
1 teaspoon cinnamon
Pinch of salt
½ cup vegetable or canola oil
½ cup honey

Preheat oven to 350 degrees. Mix dry ingredients. Stir in oil and honey. Spread on baking sheet. Bake 6 minutes. Toss. Bake 6 more minutes. Toss again. Bake a final 3-6 minutes until lightly toasted. Cool. Store in air tight container.

"The oat is the Horatio Alger of cereals, which progressed, if not from rags to riches, at least from weed to health food."
—Waverly Root, *Food*, 1980

Egg Inspirations

Now that we are advised to watch our cholesterol levels, eggs are no longer a part of our daily breakfast routine. But some studies are showing that eggs are not as bad as we've been told, especially for people with normal cholestoral levels. And when we do decide to indulge a little, why settle for plain scrambled or poached eggs? Here are some of the special egg dishes that have been favorites on Ovens menus through the years. Consider these when serving breakfast to overnight guests or when you've got a leisurely date with the Sunday paper.

Sauces mentioned below can be found in the Index.

Eggs Salsa—Toasted English muffin halves layered and briefly baked with poached eggs, salsa and grated cheddar cheese.

Eggs in Herb Butter—Pre-poached eggs simmered very gently in a pan with chopped fresh herbs and sweet butter.

Virginia's Choice—Eggs scrambled with crisp crumbled bacon and grated swiss cheese.

Eggs Florentine—Poached eggs on a bed of seasoned sautéed spinach, topped with Mornay Sauce.

Eggs Asparagus—scrambled eggs with blanched asparagus and Mornay Sauce on an English muffin.

Eggs Santa Fe—Avocado, scrambled eggs and cheddar cheese on a toasted English muffin with spicy salsa.

Eggs Mornay—Scrambled eggs and sautéed mushrooms topped with Mornay Sauce.

Eggs Benedict—Poached eggs and grilled Canadian bacon or ham on toasted English muffin halves, topped with Hollandaise Sauce.

Vegetarian Benedict—Poached eggs and tomato slices on toasted English muffin halves, topped with Hollandaise Sauce.

Eggs Robert—Lightly poached eggs baked with parmesan cheese on a layer of Mornay Sauce.

"There is always a best way of doing everything, if it be to boil an egg."
—Ralph Waldo Emerson, *Conduct of Life,* 1860

Ovens of Brittany

COOKIES, MUFFINS & BAKERY CHOICES

Triple Chip Cookies

Makes about 24 large cookies

I don't know anyone who doesn't love these cookies. They fly out of our bakeries like nobody's business. Bring them to a potluck dinner for guaranteed "oohs" and "ahs."

This recipe makes very large cookies, like the ones we sell at our bakery counters. You may wish to portion them smaller (cooking time will remain the same).

> 2 sticks (½ pound) butter, softened
> ¾ cup brown sugar
> ¾ cup sugar
> 2 eggs
> 1 teaspoon vanilla extract
> 2½ cups flour
> 1 teaspoon baking soda
> ½ teaspoon salt
> 6 ounces (about 1 cup) semisweet chocolate chips
> 3 ounces (about ½ cup) milk chocolate chips
> 3 ounces white chocolate, chopped coarsely (about ½ cup)
>   OR 3 ounces (about ½ cup) white chocolate chips

1. Preheat oven to 350 degrees. Grease cookie sheets.
2. Cream softened butter and sugars until light colored and fluffy. Lightly beat eggs and vanilla; add to butter/sugar combination. Mix until well blended.
3. In separate bowl, combine flour, soda and salt. Toss gently with your fingers. Add this to creamed mixture and stir only until flour is mixed in. Stir in all the chocolate, but don't over-mix. Dough will be somewhat stiff.
4. Drop rounded scoops (each about 2 heaping tablespoons) three inches apart on cookie sheets. Press each cookie lightly with fingertips. Bake 12-14 minutes until lightly browned. Cool.

"Man doth not live by bread alone."
—The Bible, *Deuteronomy III*

Chocolate Cadillacs

Makes 3-4 dozen

Chocolate Cadillacs are sold alongside a variety of yummy cookies in our bakery cases, but make no mistake: they are not REALLY cookies. Copious amounts of both semisweet and bittersweet chocolate, along with coffee, pecans and chocolate chips, are hidden in the guise of a richly dark, not-so-innocent-looking cookie. A Chocolate Cadillac is more a fine pastry than a simple cookie, and makes a decidedly adult treat. (But just try keeping them away from your kids!)

Compared to other cookie recipes, there is very little flour in Chocolate Cadillacs. Because the batter is not stiffened much by flour, the batter's temperature is significant, for if your kitchen is hot, the chocolaty dough will be runny and your cookies will end up looking like pancakes. A slightly chilled batter is therefore recommended.

> **1 stick (8 tablespoons) butter**
> **3 cups chocolate chips, divided**
> **4 ounces unsweetened chocolate, coarsely chopped**
> **2½ teaspoons instant coffee granules**
> **1 tablespoon hot water**
> **4 eggs**
> **1½ cups sugar**
> **2½ teaspoons vanilla**
> **¾ cup flour**
> **½ teaspoon baking powder**
> **½ teaspoon salt**
> **¼ cup pecan pieces**

1. Preheat oven to 350 degrees. Grease heavy baking sheets (do not use non-stick pans.) In microwave or double boiler, melt the butter, 1½ cups of chocolate chips and unsweetened chocolate.
2. Dissolve coffee in one tablespoon of hot water; stir it into melted chocolate. Set aside to cool slightly.
3. In large mixing bowl, cream eggs, sugar and vanilla until mixture is thickened (about 5 minutes). Stir in chocolate.
4. Sift together flour, baking powder and salt and fold into batter. Fold in remaining 1½ cups of chocolate chips and pecan pieces. If kitchen is hot or dough is very runny, refrigerate batter 15-20 minutes.
5. Drop dough by the tablespoon onto cookie sheets; bake 8-10 minutes. Cookies will be very soft when they come out of the oven; transfer carefully from baking sheets to cool.

Peanut Butter
(and Peanut Butter/Chocolate Chip)
Cookies
Makes 24-30 cookies

Go on, make a double batch.

4 tablespoons butter, softened
4 tablespoons margarine, softened
¾ cup peanut butter
½ cup sugar
½ cup brown sugar
1½ tablespoons vegetable oil
1 egg
1½ cups flour
½ teaspoon baking soda
½ cup chocolate chips (optional)
Additional sugar for pressing cookies

Preheat oven to 350 degrees. Grease cookie sheets. Cream butter, margarine, peanut butter and sugars. Stir in oil and egg. Add flour and baking soda and stir until just combined. Add chocolate chips, if desired. Drop heaping tablespoons on cookie sheets and press each cookie with a fork dipped in sugar. Bake 12-15 minutes. Cookies will be very fragile when they come out of oven; transfer carefully onto cooling racks.

Prussian Tea Cakes
Makes 2-2½ dozen

Not a cake, but a cookie, Prussian Tea Cakes are very easy and quick to make. Almonds work as well as walnuts.

2 sticks (½ pound) plus 4 tablespoons butter, well softened
⅔ cup powdered sugar
2½ teaspoons vanilla
½ teaspoon salt
2¼ cups ground walnuts
2¼ cups flour
Additional powdered sugar

Preheat oven to 350 degrees. Grease cookie sheet. Cream butter, ⅔ cup powdered sugar, vanilla and salt by hand. Stir in ground walnuts. Sift and fold in flour. Roll dough into 24-30 balls, about 2 tablespoons of dough for each ball. Flatten bottoms slightly as you place them on cookie sheet. Bake 17 minutes. Cookies are very delicate when they come out of oven. Roll in powdered sugar while still warm, then cool completely.

"Always get up from the table feeling as if you could still eat a penny bun."
—Sir Hugh Casson & Joyce Grenfell, *Nanny Says,* 1972

Bailey's Corn-Oat Muffins
Makes 14-16 muffins

Not surprisingly, some of our best recipes come from "regulars," special customers who have a kind of second home at one of the Ovens. Some will order the same thing time after time while others know each item on the menu as well as the cooks. Regulars feel like family to us, and just like family, we love them for their support and honest input.

Years ago one of the regulars at the Ovens on Monroe Street gave us a muffin recipe that had been passed down through her family's generations. It's a homey, satisfying muffin with a coconuty crunch. You'll like Bailey's Corn-Oat Muffins with fresh fruit for breakfast, or as a go-with for any meal of the day.

Special Notes: Even a novice baker can get great results with muffins by following a few simple rules: start with a hot oven and take care to avoid overmixing the batter. Using heavy aluminum pans (not non-stick) gives the best results.

- 1 ½ cups flour
- 1 ½ teaspoons baking powder
- 1 teaspoon baking soda
- 1 teaspoon salt
- ½ cup brown sugar
- ⅔ cup cornmeal
- ⅔ cup chopped walnuts
- ⅔ cup quick-cooking oats
- ⅔ cup dried coconut flakes
- 2 eggs
- 1 ½ cups buttermilk
- 5 tablespoons butter, melted

Preheat oven to 400 degrees; grease muffins pans. Sift together flour, baking powder, baking soda, and salt. Stir in brown sugar, cornmeal, walnuts, oats, and coconut. In a large bowl, lightly beat eggs and mix in buttermilk and melted butter. Add dry mixture to the wet, and quickly stir until just blended. Do not beat or overmix. Fill muffin cups nearly full. Bake 15 minutes, until toothpick inserted in center of muffins comes out clean. Cool a few mintues and remove from pan.

Coffee Chocolate Chip Muffins
Makes 16-20 muffins

When is a cupcake also a muffin? Coffee Chocolate Chip Muffins are a variation on a mocha theme that work as a dessert or as a bread. Easy to make and not-too-sweet, they fit naturally into any meal (or snack) of the day. So when is a cupcake also a muffin? When you decide to call it one!

6 ounces (12 tablespoons) butter, softened
¼ cup sugar
½ cup brown sugar
3 tablespoons instant coffee granules
1 ½ teaspoons vanilla
1 egg
1 ½ cups flour
1 tablespoon baking powder
⅛ teaspoon salt
½ cup milk
½ cup chocolate chips

Preheat oven to 375 degrees; line muffin cups with paper liners. In a large bowl, cream the softened butter, sugars, coffee and vanilla. Mix in egg. In a separate bowl, sift flour, baking powder and salt. Alternately stir flour mixture and milk into creamed mixture. Do not overmix. Stir in chocolate chips. Fill muffin cups nearly full; bake 15-20 minutes, until toothpick inserted in center of muffins comes out clean.

Blueberry Muffins
Makes 12-16 muffins

Double the recipe and freeze the extras for a convenient breakfast on hurried mornings. Simply thaw and heat in your microwave or toaster oven.

1¾ cups flour
½ cup whole wheat flour
1 cup brown sugar
1 tablespoon baking powder
1 teaspoon salt
3½ tablespoons cold butter
1½ cups blueberries (fresh, or frozen and thawed)
2 eggs
1 cup milk

1. Preheat oven to 375 degrees. Grease muffin pans.
2. In food processor or by hand, mix flours, brown sugar, baking powder and salt. Cut cold butter into small pieces and, using the pulse button on the processor or a pastry cutter, cut butter into dry ingredients until mixture is texture of coarse cornmeal.
3. Remove to a bowl (if you have been using food processor) and stir in blueberries.
4. Mix eggs and milk, then stir into dry ingredients until just blended. Do not overmix.
5. Divide batter into muffin cups, filling almost full. Bake 20-25 minutes until toothpick inserted in center of muffin comes out clean.

Oat Bran Muffins
Makes 12-18 muffins

2 cups flour
1 cup brown sugar
1½ teaspoons baking powder
1½ teaspoons baking soda
½ teaspoon salt
1½ cups oat bran
1 egg
1½ cups milk

⅓ cup vegetable oil
2 tablespoons molasses
¼ cup raisins
¼ cup pitted, chopped dates

Preheat oven to 375 degrees. Grease muffin tins. Sift together the first five ingredients, then stir in oat bran. In separate bowl, mix egg, milk, oil and molasses. Stir wet ingredients into dry ingredients. Fold in raisins and dates. Fill muffin tins nearly full. Bake 20-25 minutes, until toothpick inserted in center of muffin comes out clean.

Lauren's Pumpkin Bran Muffins
Makes 12 muffins

1 cup all-purpose flour
1 cup brown sugar
⅓ cup whole wheat flour
¼ cup wheat bran
¾ teaspoon baking soda
½ teaspoon ground cinnamon
¼ teaspoon ground allspice
¼ teaspoon ground ginger
¼ teaspoon ground nutmeg
¼ teaspoon ground cloves
¼ teaspoon salt
1 can (16 ounces) solid pack pumpkin
3 eggs
2 tablespoons molasses

Preheat oven to 375 degrees. Grease muffin tins or line tins with muffin papers. Sift together white flour and brown sugar. Stir in whole wheat flour, bran, baking soda and seasonings. In separate bowl combine remaining ingredients. Stir into flour mixture. Divide into 12 muffin cups. Bake 20-25 minutes.

English Tea Scones
Makes 8-10 scones

English tea usually conjures up notions of cream-filled pastries, delicate china and dainty cucumber sandwiches, but these scones are simply hearty and *good*. The dough is rolled very thick and if you don't have a biscuit cutter to make the scones round, cut the dough into triangles with a sharp knife instead. Serve with sweet cream butter and preserves.

    2 cups whole wheat flour
    1 ½ cups all-purpose flour
    4 teaspoons baking powder
    1 teaspoon salt
    ¼ pound (8 tablespoons) cold butter, in small pieces
    1 cup chopped dates
    2 eggs
    ½ cup plus one tablespoon milk (plus additional milk, if required)
    ¼ cup honey
    Additional flour

1. Preheat oven to 400 degrees; grease a cookie sheet.
2. Mix together flours, baking powder and salt. Cut in butter until it is the size of small peas. Stir in dates.
3. Beat eggs lightly, and hold about 1 tablespoon of egg aside for later. Add milk and honey to the larger amount of egg. Stir egg and flour mixtures together until just combined. If necessary, add a little more milk to hold mixture together. Do not overmix!
4. Turn dough onto a floured surface and gently press it together. Press or roll to a thickness of 1½ inches. Cut with a 3-inch biscuit cutter. Mix reserved tablespoon of egg with a little water and brush top of each scone with this "eggwash."
5. Place scones on cookie sheet and bake 15 to 20 minutes until the tops are medium brown. Remove from pan and cool.

Jesse's Almond Buttermilk Scones
Makes 8 three-inch scones

Easy, light and excellent. These scones are *notably* delicious. Serve warm with butter, honey, jam or all three.

3 cups flour
½ cup sugar
½ cup sliced almonds
1 scant tablespoon baking powder
½ teaspoon salt
2 tablespoons cold butter, cut into small pieces
2 eggs
¾ cup buttermilk
½ teaspoon almond extract
Additional flour

Preheat oven to 350 degrees. Grease baking pan. Mix flour, sugar, almonds, baking powder and salt. Cut in butter until size of tiny peas. Combine eggs, buttermilk and almond extract; stir into flour mixture until just combined. Turn onto floured surface; press gently into a round 1½ inches thick. Do not over-work. Cut into 3-inch rounds with biscuit cutter; place on pan and bake 20 minutes. Serve warm. Freeze any leftovers as they dry out quickly.

"The lion and the unicorn
Were fighting for the crown;
The lion beat the unicorn
All round the town.
Some gave them white bread,
And some gave them brown;
And some gave them plum-cake,
And sent them out of town."
Nursery Rhyme from *Useful Transactions in Philosophy* by William King, 1708-1709

Oatmeal Tea Cake
Serves 12-16

Looking for a recipe that doesn't require a trip to the store for special ingredients? Oatmeal Tea Cake is just the thing for a rainy morning; it's made from basic ingredients found in most cupboards and has a warming, wholesome appeal. Serve it as a coffeecake with powdered sugar sifted over the surface or dress it up for tea time with sweet frosting. Or how about drizzling pure maple syrup over a warm slice? Oatmeal never had it so good!

1¼ cups quick-cooking oats
1¾ cups boiling water
6 tablespoons margarine, softened
4 tablespoons butter, softened
1¼ cups white sugar
1¼ cups brown sugar
3 eggs
1½ teaspoons vanilla
1¼ teaspoons baking soda
½ teaspoon salt
1¼ teaspoons cinnamon
½ teaspoon nutmeg
2½ cups flour

Preheat oven to 350 degrees; grease and flour an 8-by-8 inch baking dish. In medium bowl, pour the boiling water over oats and set aside to soak. In large bowl, cream margarine, butter and sugars. Add eggs, vanilla, baking soda, salt, cinnamon and nutmeg. Stir in oats/water mixture. Stir in flour. Pour batter into pan. Bake 50 minutes, or until toothpick inserted in center comes out clean. Serve warm or at room temperature and see above for serving suggestions.

Ovens of Brittany

PASTRIES

Caramel Walnut Torte
Serves 10-14

Absolute heaven! Thick, rich, gooey caramel is crammed with walnuts and surrounded by a chocolate-glazed crust. I've never seen anyone eat this extravagance without moaning just a little!

Caramel Walnut Torte was created by Amy Nadeau and Jeanette Dykema, two long-time pastry chefs with the Ovens of Brittany. In a search for dynamite desserts a prize was offered to the baker who could come up with the most temptingly delicious treat. Amy and Jeanette combined their ideas and delivered this prize-winning knock-out. It's the best!

Filling Ingredients:
    1 cup sugar
    ¼ cup light corn syrup
    4½ tablespoons butter
    ⅔ cup heavy cream
    2 cups chopped walnuts
    2 teaspoons honey
    1½ teaspoons kirsch (cherry liqueur)

Other Ingredients:
    Flour
    One recipe Tart Dough (page 106), chilled
    Egg white
    6 ounces semisweet chocolate, chopped
    4 tablespoons butter, cut into small pieces
    Walnut halves (optional)

To make filling:
1. Combine sugar, 2½ tablespoons water and corn syrup in heavy saucepan. Cook over low heat a few minutes, stirring occasionally, until sugar has dissolved. Brush sides of pan with moistened brush to wash down any sugar crystals that have formed.
2. Cover pan, raise heat to medium and cook 10-15 minutes until mixture is caramelized or has turned an amber color. Do not stir while it is cooking, but swirl the pan occasionally.
3. Add 4½ tablespoons butter and stir until dissolved, then add cream and walnuts. Boil gently until mixture reaches 225 degrees. Cool for about 10 minutes. Stir in honey and kirsch. Cool to room temperature.

To assemble, bake and glaze:

4. Preheat oven to 350 degrees. Grease and flour an 8-inch by 1½-inch cake pan.
5. Working on a floured surface, divide the tart dough into two portions, one about 9 ounces and the other about 6 ounces. Roll the larger piece into a round that will fit into the bottom and sides of the pan. Press this round gently into the pan and brush all surfaces with egg white.
6. Pour cooled filling into the pan. Roll out the other portion of dough to fit the top. Brush the top edge of the bottom crust with more egg white. Lay the second round of dough on the top and press the edges together to form a seal.
7. Bake 30 minutes until surface is lightly browned.
8. Meanwhile, make glaze by melting chocolate and 4 tablespoons butter together in microwave or over simmering water. Cool to room temperature.
9. When torte is baked, cool completely. Run a sharp knife around the sides of the torte and de-pan. Chill thoroughly. Spread the glaze evenly around the sides and top of the torte. (If glaze is too firm to spread, warm in microwave or over simmering water.) You may garnish by placing walnut halves around the top edge of the torte. Chill for 10-20 minutes to set the glaze. Serve chilled or at room temperature.

"The dessert is said to be to the dinner what the madrigal is to literature—
it is the light poetry of the kitchen."
—George Ellwanger, *Pleasures of the Table,* 1903

"Bring on the dessert. I think I am about to die."
—Pierette Brillat-Savarin, last words, 1911

Tart Dough

Makes one crust

1 ½ cups flour
¼ teaspoon salt
⅓ cup sugar
6 tablespoons cold butter, cut into small pieces
3 egg yolks, lightly beaten
½ teaspoon vanilla

1. Mix together flour, salt and sugar in food processor or by hand. Cut in the butter pieces until mixture resembles meal and there are no butter chunks.
2. Combine egg yolks, vanilla, and two tablespoons of water and mix with the flour until it just begins to hold together when you press it in your hand. (If you are using a food processor, take care not to overmix.) Add more water only if necessary to hold the dough together.
3. Put mixture on table top and, using the heel of your hand, press sections of the dough against the table surface. Now it will hold together easily. Press and form the dough into a flat round; wrap and chill it at least one hour before proceeding with dessert recipe.

Special Notes: You will have leftover egg whites with this recipe but don't throw them away! They freeze very well and can be used in many ways. Here are some ideas: Use them as a binder for meatloaves, stuffings, or casseroles. For a lower cholesterol breakfast, substitute them for some of the whole eggs in your omelettes or scrambled eggs. Egg whites are essential when making lemon meringue pie or macaroons. Strips of cooked egg whites are delicious in a stirfry or in fried rice. Finally, brush egg white on homemade bread before baking for a shiny look, or use a little to seal filled pastries and turnovers.

"Pastry-making . . . is one of the most important branches of the culinary sciences.
It unceasingly occupies itself with ministering pleasure to the sight as well as the taste."
—Mrs. Isabella Beeton, *The Book of Household Management,* 1880

Tarte au Citron

Serves 8

This flavorful dessert recipe came to us from a cooking class attended in France many years ago by one of our pastry chefs. I think of it as a very elegant version of the lemon bar, a bit like Eliza Doolittle after her transformation by Professor Higgins . . . beautiful, refined, but with a spunky tartness.

To make Tarte au Citron you will need a flan pan, which is a shallow pan with fluted sides and a removable bottom. (Hold this pan from the sides, and not the bottom or you will be "left hanging.") If you don't own a flan pan, a shallow pie pan of approximately the same dimensions will work.

> **One recipe Tart Dough (page 106), chilled**
> **Flour**
> **Uncooked, dried beans (for weighting the crust)**
> **Juice and finely grated peel of 1 small lemon**
> **¼ cup ground sliced almonds**
> **3½ tablespoons butter, melted**
> **3 eggs**
> **½ cup sugar, divided**
> **Powdered sugar**

1. To bake tart dough, preheat oven to 350 degrees. Grease a round 9½-inch flan pan (with removable bottom). Roll out dough on a floured surface so that it is about one half inch larger all around than the pan. Line pan with dough, folding excess back into pan and pressing it into the sides. Line dough with foil and fill with uncooked dried beans. Bake 10 minutes. Remove foil and beans and bake an additional 3 minutes, or until crust looks dry. (If crust puffs a little, pierce it gently with a toothpick.) Remove pan from oven; leave oven on and make filling while crust cools.

2. To make filling: Combine grated lemon peel, lemon juice, ground almonds and melted butter. Set aside. Separate eggs into two dry, grease-free bowls. Beat egg yolks on high speed with electric beater, slowly adding all but one tablespoon of the sugar. Beat until yolks became thick and pale yellow and a ribbon forms over the surface of the batter when you lift a beater out. Stir in lemon mixture and set aside. Clean and dry beaters, then beat egg whites on high speed. As they begin to thicken, gradually add the remaining one tablespoon of sugar. Continue beating for a minute or two until whites round up when you lift out a beater but do not form stiff peaks. Gently stir a quarter of the whipped egg whites into batter, then fold in remaining egg whites. Pour batter into cooled tart shell.

3. Bake 20-25 minutes until an indentation is left when you press the tart with your finger. Cool. Sprinkle with sifted powered sugar and serve.

Pots de Creme
Serves 5-6

This extravagant custard combines chocolate, egg yolks, sweet cream and the cherry liqueur known as kirsch. The satiny smooth, ultra-thick texture and deep chocolate flavor are unforgettable. Serve Pots de Creme (pronounced poh-de-krehm) in small portions, perhaps in champagne coupes, with a dollop of whipped cream. It really is an outrageously delicious dessert and given the ingredients, that's about the only excuse there is for eating it!

½ pound semisweet chocolate, cut into small pieces
   ***OR* 1 package (8 ounces) semisweet chocolate chips**
1 cup heavy cream
1 cup half-and-half
9 egg yolks
2 tablespoons kirsch (cherry liqueur)
Whipped cream and chocolate shavings (optional)

1. Melt chocolate in microwave or double boiler. Set aside.
2. Heat heavy cream and half-and-half in heavy saucepan. Meanwhile, whisk egg yolks lightly in a mixing bowl.
3. When cream mixture has just reached a boil, pour it slowly into yolks, whisking as you pour. Return mixture to pan and continue whisking over medium low heat until mixture begins to thicken. This will only take a few minutes. Do not overcook or the eggs will scramble.
4. When mixture has thickened to the consistency of heavy cream and coats the back of a spoon, pour it back into the mixing bowl. Whisk in melted chocolate, then the kirsch.
5. When mixture is smooth, pour it into a small pitcher, or a gravy bowl with a lip. Pour custard into individual glasses or serving dishes. About one half cup is sufficient for each serving as this is an exceedingly rich dessert. Cover each with plastic wrap and refrigerate at least two hours before serving. Whipped cream is a perfect complement to the custard; a few shavings of chocolate adds extra flair.

Note: True chocolate fanatics love almost any form or flavor that their favorite vice is coupled with, so take note that the kirsch in this recipe can be honorably substituted with coffee- or orange-flavored liqueur or your own personal preference.

Lemon Poppyseed Cheesecake
Serves 12-14

Crust Ingredients:
>1½ cups graham cracker crumbs
>3 tablespoons butter

Filling Ingredients:
>2 pounds (or four 8-ounce packages) cream cheese, softened
>1 cup sugar
>2 tablespoons flour
>2½ teaspoons vanilla extract
>5 eggs
>½ cup heavy cream
>Juice and finely grated peel of 1 large lemon
>2 tablespoons fresh lemon juice
>⅓ cup poppyseeds
>Candied lemon slices (optional)

1. To make crust, melt butter and combine with graham cracker crumbs. Press mixture into the bottom and up the sides a little of a 9-inch springform pan. Refrigerate crust until ready to bake cheesecake.
2. Preheat oven to 350 degrees. To make filling, cream softened cream cheese with electric beaters for several minutes. Scrape the sides of the bowl several times during this process.
3. Add sugar, flour, and vanilla, and beat until smooth. Add eggs and continue beating and scraping down the sides of the bowl until all is smooth. Mix in cream, again until smooth. Stir in juice and grated peel of a large lemon, plus the additional lemon juice and the poppyseeds.
4. Pour filling into crust and bake until just set, about 50-55 minutes. A reading of 160 degrees on an instant thermometer placed in the center of the cheesecake is your best assurance that it is done correctly. Other signs are that the surface will be very lightly browned, and the middle of the cheese-cake won't jiggle loosely when moved.
5. Remove cheesecake from oven and immediately run a thin-bladed knife all around the edges. Place a large lid or flat pan on top of the cheesecake pan and let cool. This will help prevent the cheesecake from cracking.
6. Cheesecake tastes best after it has chilled overnight and then is returned to room temperature. Remove outer ring of pan and decorate cheesecake if desired (tiny candied lemon slices are lovely). This dessert goes a long way and keeps very well.

Shorewood's Gingerbread With Honey Rum Sauce

Serves 16-24

This cozy gingerbread came from a recipe titled "Mary Washington's Gingerbread" and has been served at the Shorewood Ovens for many holiday seasons. Serve this spicy cake slightly warm, topped with a spoonful of hot honey rum sauce and a dollop of sweetened whipped cream. It makes winter worthwhile.

> 6 ounces (12 tablespoons) butter, softened
> 4 eggs
> 1 cup honey
> 1 cup dark molasses
> 4½ cups flour
> 1 tablespoon ground ginger
> 1½ teaspoons nutmeg
> 1½ teaspoons cinnamon
> 1½ teaspoons cream of tartar
> ¾ cup milk
> ½ cup rum
> Finely grated peel and juice from 2 oranges
> 1½ teaspoons baking soda
> 1 tablespoon warm water

Honey Rum Sauce Ingredients:
> 1 cup honey
> 1/16 teaspoon salt
> 2 tablespoons cornstarch
> 2 tablespoons butter
> ½ cup rum

1. Preheat oven to 350 degrees. Grease and flour a 9-by-13 inch baking pan. Cream butter and eggs, add honey and molasses and continue to cream until smooth.
2. Sift together flour, ginger, nutmeg, cinnamon and cream of tartar.
3. Add flour and milk alternately to creamed mixture, stirring well after each addition. Add rum, grated orange peel and orange juice. Dissolve baking soda in 1 tablespoon of warm water and stir into batter.

4. Pour batter into pan and bake 45-55 minutes, until toothpick inserted in center comes out clean. Serve warm with hot honey rum sauce.
5. To make sauce: combine honey with ¾ cup water and the salt in a saucepan; bring to boil; cook 3-4 minutes. Dissolve cornstarch in ½ cup of water; add to mixture; cook until thick and transparent. Remove from heat and stir in butter and rum.

Carrot Cake With
Cream Cheese Frosting
Serves 16-20

Here's a cinnamony Carrot Cake, rich with pineapple, walnuts and a snow-white cream cheese frosting. It's so good that it's not unusual for customers to select it as their wedding cake.

> 1 cup vegetable oil
> 1½ cups sugar
> 3 eggs
> 1 pound carrots, cleaned and grated
> 1 can (8 ounces) crushed pineapple, drained
> ½ cup walnuts
> 1¾ cups flour
> 1½ teaspoons cinnamon
> 1½ teaspoons baking powder
> 1¼ teaspoons baking soda
> ½ teaspoon salt

Frosting Ingredients:
> 1 package (8 ounces) cream cheese, softened
> 2½ tablespoons margarine or softened butter
> ⅓ cup powdered sugar, sifted

1. Preheat oven to 350 degrees. Grease and flour a 9-by-13 inch baking pan. Cream oil, sugar and eggs. Add carrots, drained pineapple and walnuts. Sift together then fold in the flour, cinnamon, baking powder, baking soda and salt. Pour batter into pan; bake until toothpick inserted in center comes out clean, about 40 minutes.
2. To make frosting: Cream together cream cheese and margarine or butter. Beat in sifted powdered sugar. Frost cake when it is completely cooled.

Queen of Sheba Torte

Serves 12-14

Perhaps more than any other dessert, Queen of Sheba Torte epitomizes the grandeur of an Ovens of Brittany pastry. This currant-studded chocolate torte is flavored with brandy, almonds, and walnuts, and is enveloped with chocolate glaze. Whipped cream is the natural accent, and a cup of cappuccino completes the picture.

Torte Ingredients:
>6 ounces semisweet chocolate, coarsely chopped
>⅓ cup currants
>3 tablespoons brandy
>6 ounces (12 tablespoons) butter, softened
>1 cup plus 1 tablespoon sugar, divided
>1 teaspoon almond extract
>5 eggs
>¼ cup sliced almonds, minced
>¼ cup minced walnuts
>1 cup flour

Other Ingredients:
>6 ounces semisweet chocolate, coarsely chopped
>   OR 1 cup chocolate chips
>4 tablespoons butter, in small pieces
>Additional sliced almonds (optional)

1. Grease and flour a round cake pan, 8 inches in diameter and at least 2 inches high. Preheat oven to 350 degrees. Melt the first 6 ounces of chocolate in microwave or double boiler. Set aside to cool. Heat together currants and brandy (40 seconds if using a microwave oven). Set aside.
2. In large mixing bowl, cream 6 ounces softened butter and 1 cup of sugar until light and fluffy. Stir in almond extract. Separate eggs, setting whites aside in a clean bowl and beating yolks into butter/sugar mixture. Stir the melted chocolate, currant/brandy mixture and nuts into the butter mixture.
3. Beat egg whites until they form soft peaks. Add remaining tablespoon of sugar and continue to beat until stiff but not dry. Stir a blob of egg whites into chocolate batter, then gently and alternately fold in remaining egg whites and flour.
4. Pour batter into cake pan; bake 30-40 minutes. Torte is done if it jiggles a little in very center when you shake it and the sides have shrunk away from the pan. Also, a crust will have formed over top of whole cake, and a toothpick inserted in the center will come out slightly gooey.

5. Cool cake for 15-20 minutes, then de-pan and cool completely. Meanwhile, make chocolate glaze by melting remaining 6 ounces of chocolate (or 1 cup chocolate chips) and the butter pieces in a microwave or double boiler. Glaze should be cooled to room temperature, but should still be spreadable.
6. Spread glaze evenly around the sides and top of torte. Garnish with sliced almonds, if desired, and chill briefly to set the glaze. Serve at room temperature.

Farm Cakes

Makes 16 cupcakes

These curiously named cupcakes are super-moist and cocoa-rich, with a cream cheese accent. Perhaps they get their name from the old-fashioned addition of a little vinegar to the batter, which serves to enhance the chocolaty goodness.

> 3 ounces cream cheese, softened
> 1 egg
> 1 cup plus 3 tablespoons sugar, divided
> ⅛ teaspoon salt
> ½ cup chocolate chips
> 1½ cups flour
> 6 tablespoons cocoa powder (unsweetened)
> 1½ teaspoons baking soda
> 1 cup water
> 6 tablespoons oil
> ½ teaspoon vanilla
> 3 tablespoons cider vinegar

Preheat oven to 375 degrees. Line muffin tins with paper liners. Cream the cream cheese, egg, 3 tablespoons sugar and salt with an electric mixer. Fold in chocolate chips and set this mixture aside. Sift together flour, remaining 1 cup sugar, cocoa and baking soda. In separate bowl, mix water, oil, vanilla and vinegar. Add water/oil mixture to the flour mixture; combine in a few swift strokes. Do not overmix. Batter will be lumpy. Divide into muffin cups, each three-quarters full. Top each with a scant teaspoon of the cream cheese mixture. Bake 18-20 minutes. The cream cheese mixture will have "sunk" into the cupcakes somewhat. Cool to room temperature.

Chocolate Truffle Torte
Serves 12-16

If you are a chocoholic, this is the dessert of your dreams. Three layers of a rich chocolate-almond torte are generously filled with chocolate mousse and covered with a dark mocha glaze. The cake is baked in an oblong pan then cut into three rectangles and "stacked." What an impressively dramatic effect as you slice through the torte to reveal the decadent layers. Chocolate Truffle Torte takes some effort, so make it when there's something extra-special to celebrate. Or make it for someone who really deserves it. Like yourself.

Torte Ingredients:
> 5½ ounces bittersweet chocolate, cut into small chunks
> 1 teaspoon instant coffee dissolved in 4 teaspoons hot water
>   OR 4 teaspoons strong fresh-brewed coffee
> 1 teaspoon vanilla
> 11 tablespoons butter, softened
> 1¼ cups powdered sugar, divided
> 6 eggs, separated into yolks and whites
> 1⅓ cups ground almond slivers
> ¼ cup flour
> 1 teaspoon baking powder

Mousse Ingredients:
> 6 ounces semisweet chocolate, cut into small chunks
> 12 tablespoons butter, cut into small chunks
> 1½ tablespoons rum or other liqueur
> ¾ cup heavy cream

Other Ingredients:
> Double recipe of Mocha Glaze (recipe follows)
> Ground or whole almond slivers

1. *To make torte:* Preheat oven to 350 degrees. You'll need a jelly roll pan (a cookie sheet with sides) at least 9½ by 13 inches in size. Grease pan and line with parchment paper *OR* generously grease and flour it.
2. Melt 5½ ounces bittersweet chocolate. Stir in hot coffee and vanilla. Set aside.
3. Cream softened butter and ¾ cup of powdered sugar. Add egg yolks one at a time, stirring after each addition. Stir in chocolate mixture.
4. Combine almonds, flour and baking powder and add to chocolate mixture.
5. In clean bowl, whip egg whites until they begin to peak. Slowly add remaining ½ cup of powdered sugar and continue whipping until stiff peaks form.

6. Lighten chocolate batter by stirring in one quarter of the whipped egg whites. Gently but thoroughly fold in remaining egg whites. Smooth batter lightly into pan. Bake 20-22 minutes, until cake begins to pull away from edges of pan.
7. While cake is still warm but not hot, place large board or tray over it and invert cake onto board. (If you have not used parchment paper you will first need to loosen cake gently all around the bottom with an egg-lifter.) Cool completely and remove paper. Trim edges and cut cake into three equal-sized rectangles. (Cake layers may be wrapped airtight and refrigerated or frozen until ready to assemble.)
8. *To make mousse filling:* Melt 6 ounces chocolate and butter chunks together. Stir in rum. In a separate bowl, whip heavy cream until stiff peaks form. Fold whipped cream into chocolate mixture. Refrigerate until ready to assemble.
9. *To assemble and glaze:* Prepare double recipe of mocha glaze if you have not already done so. Layer and stack cake pieces with mousse (three cake layers and two mousse layers); smooth the edges. Freeze torte 30 minutes, then spread glaze over sides and top. Decorate with ground or whole almond slivers. Refrigerate to set the glaze, and keep refrigerated until 30 minutes before serving. This torte looks stunning with an accent of fresh flowers.

Mocha Glaze

Makes about 1 cup

¼ cup heavy cream
1 tablespoon sugar
1 tablespoon butter
4 ounces semisweet chocolate, cut into small chunks *OR*
  ¾ cup chocolate chips
1 teaspoon instant coffee, dissolved in 3 tablespoons hot water
  OR 3 tablespoons strong, hot fresh-brewed coffee

Combine cream, sugar and butter in small saucepan and bring to boil. Boil one minute, turn off heat, add chocolate and whisk until glaze is shiny and smooth. Whisk in hot coffee. Glaze can be stored in refrigerator for several days. Reheat gently in microwave or over simmering water to return to spreading consistency.

Marble Cheese Torte
Serves 12-14

Marble Cheese Torte is a velvety chocolate-marbled cheesecake on a walnut cookie crust with a smooth-as-silk chocolate glaze. If that sounds mouth-watering to you, you're in good company, for it has been a popular choice on Ovens menus for so long that it could be called a classic. Don't worry about cracks in this cheesecake. After baking and chilling the torte, the top of the cheesecake is pressed to even out the surface, and the chocolate glaze hides all imperfections. This is one of those desserts that tastes better the second day.

Crust Ingredients:
4 tablespoons butter, softened
2 tablespoons packed brown sugar
¾ cup flour
¼ cup chopped walnuts

Other Ingredients:
2 pounds (or four 8-ounce packages) cream cheese, softened
1 cup sugar
2 tablespoons flour
2½ teaspoons vanilla extract
5 eggs
½ cup heavy cream
1 recipe Mocha Glaze (page 115), divided
2 tablespoons finely chopped walnuts (optional garnish)

1. To make crust: Preheat oven to 350 degrees. Cream butter and brown sugar. Mix in flour and walnuts. Press dough into bottom of a 9-inch springform pan. Bake 15 minutes, then allow to cool while you make filling.
2. To make filling: Cream softened cream cheese with electric beaters for several minutes, scraping sides of bowl often. Add sugar, flour and vanilla and beat until smooth. Add eggs and continue beating and scraping down sides of bowl until smooth. Mix in cream.
3. If you have not already done so, prepare the Mocha Glaze. Glaze should be just warm enough to pour, but not hot.
4. Pour cream cheese filling into crust in pan. Drizzle 3 tablespoons of glaze over surface of filling, then swirl the filling with a skewer or thin-bladed knife, crisscrossing the glaze throughout. (Reserve remaining glaze until later.) Bake 50-55 minutes until set. (Instant thermometer inserted in center of cheesecake should read 160 degrees.) Cool to room temperature then chill thoroughly. (Torte can be held overnight and finished the following day.)
5. Press down all over top of cheesecake with fingertips to even out surface. Press together any cracks. If necessary, reheat glaze to spreading consistency. Pour glaze over the surface and spread evenly. Chill to set glaze. To serve, run knife around edge of cheesecake; remove ring. Sprinkle chopped walnuts around outer rim of top surface, if desired.

Plum Cake
Serves 16-20

Though Plum Cake is essentially a holiday dessert, we make it all year long to help satisfy the demand for its melodiously spicy flavor. The secret to its extraordinary moistness is to gently poke holes in the still-warm cake and spoon over the buttermilk glaze, allowing it to slowly seep into the fruit-and-nut-speckled pastry. Whatever you do, don't let the addition of prunes throw you. Even diehard prune-haters are known to gush over this one.

>   1½ cups oil
>   2 cups sugar
>   4 eggs
>   1½ cups pitted prunes
>   2 cups chopped walnuts
>   2 teaspoons vanilla
>   3 cups flour
>   1 tablespoon cinnamon
>   2 teaspoons salt
>   2 teaspoons baking soda
>   1 teaspoon nutmeg
>   1½ cups buttermilk

Glaze Ingredients:
>   4 tablespoons butter
>   ¾ cup sugar
>   ⅓ cup buttermilk
>   ½ tablespoon dark corn syrup
>   ½ teaspoon baking soda
>   ½ teaspoon vanilla

1. Preheat oven to 350 degrees. Grease and flour a 9-by-13 inch baking pan.
2. In large bowl, cream oil and sugar with electric mixer 3 minutes. Beat in eggs.
3. Chop prunes by flouring them lightly and chopping with sharp knife. Add prunes, walnuts and vanilla to creamed mixture.
4. Sift together flour, cinnamon, salt, baking soda and nutmeg. Stir flour mixture and buttermilk, alternately, into creamed mixture, one third of each at a time. With each addition, stir only until just combined.
5. Pour batter into pan; bake 45-55 minutes, until toothpick inserted in center of cake comes out clean. Meanwhile, make glaze: Combine glaze ingredients in saucepan and heat almost to a boil. Do not let it boil. Set aside.
6. When cake has cooled 15 minutes, poke deep holes over the entire surface using a meat fork or a skewer. Stir glaze and spoon it slowly over the cake, allowing it to soak in. Serve warm or cool, with or without whipped cream.

Sour Cream Apple or Cherry Bars

Makes 20-30 bars

The restaurant world sometimes speaks a language all its own. In the busy rush of the day, phrases like "we've run out of the Mediterranean Pasta Salad" becomes "86 the Med," and "immerse the cooked vegetables in ice water" turns into "shock the vegies." Everybody and everything seems to acquire a nickname, whether it's a simple shortening of a title ("FO" for a bowl of French Onion Soup) or a clever take-off on someone's unique traits ("Stitch" for the guy whose early experiences with a chef's knife were both fearless and unlucky, and "Sarge" for the kitchen manager who braves the onslaught of incoming brunch orders with thunderous good humor).

One hapless newcomer, whose real name (Brian) was shared by at least three other employees, was invited to distinguish himself from the crowd and invent his own moniker. Using his corny (and what was to become notorious) wit, he must have been a bit desperate when, inspired by a package of snack cakes, he dubbed himself "Little Debbie." Brian is not a little man, and he doesn't look anything like a deb, and even though he later filled the respectable position of chef, the name stuck. I suppose it's no consolation that he has no one to blame but himself.

Some food service jargon is universal, but even the unique lingo of individual restaurants usually evolves from a simple need for efficiency. And, since we're proud of our labors, we're also fond of the labels we attach to them. The recipe below may yield Sour Cream Apple Bars for you, but to me they'll always be "Scap." (And if made with cherries instead of apples? Why, that's "Cherry Scap!")

Crust Ingredients:
> 1½ cups flour
> ⅓ cup sugar
> 1½ teaspoons cinnamon
> ¾ teaspoon salt
> 8 tablespoons (1 stick) cold butter, cut into small pieces
> 2 tablespoons orange juice or apple cider

Filling Ingredients:
- 1 egg, lightly beaten
- 1½ cups sour half-and-half (a lower fat sour cream)
- ¾ cup sugar
- ¼ cup flour
- 2 teaspoons vanilla
- 1 teasoon lemon juice
- ½ teaspoon salt
- 4 cups peeled, chopped apples *OR* pitted sour cherries

Topping Ingredients:
- ½ cup flour
- ⅓ cup brown sugar
- ¼ teaspoon cinnamon
- ¼ teaspoon salt
- 8 tablespoons (1 stick) cold butter, cut into small pieces
- 1 cup chopped walnuts

1. Preheat oven to 350 degrees. Grease a 10-by-15 inch jelly roll pan (a cookie sheet with sides) or a 9-by-13 inch baking pan. To make crust, mix dry ingredients together. Cut in butter until mixture is of very fine texture. Mix in liquid until just combined. Pat into pan.
2. To make filling, combine all ingredients except the fruit. Fold in fruit, spread over crust. Bake 30 minutes. (Topping is added at this point and bars are baked further.)
3. To make topping, combine flour, sugar, cinnamon and salt. Cut in butter until size of peas. Stir in walnuts. Refrigerate topping until bars have baked the first 30 minutes.
4. Sprinkle topping over partially-baked filling; bake an additional 10-15 minutes. Cool and serve.

"No matter how creative a cook you are, you will always be handicapped in the kitchen by mediocre ingredients."
—Perla Meyers, *From Market to Kitchen Cookbook*

Fudge Nut Oat Brownies

Makes 20-30 bars

2½ cups quick-cooking oats
2¼ cups flour
¾ cup white sugar
¾ cup brown sugar
1½ cups chopped walnuts, divided
1½ teaspoons baking soda
1 teaspoon salt
12 tablespoons cold butter, cut into small pieces
2 eggs
2 teaspoons vanilla, divided
1 small can (5 ounces) evaporated milk
3 tablespoons butter
2 tablespoons dark corn syrup
2½ cups chocolate chips

1. Preheat oven to 350 degrees. Grease a 10-by-15 inch cookie sheet with sides or a baking pan with similar dimensions.
2. Combine oats, flour, sugars, ¾ cup of the walnuts, baking soda and salt. Cut in the cold butter pieces with a pastry cutter or two knives until size of small peas.
3. Add eggs and 1 teaspoon of vanilla and mix by hand until mixture just begins to hold together. Do not overmix or mixture will become too soft and sticky.
4. Press half the dough onto bottom of baking pan. (If mixture has become sticky, dip fingers in flour and then proceed to press dough.) Set remaining half of dough aside.
5. Heat milk, 3 tablespoons of butter, and corn syrup together. When milk boils, turn heat off, add chocolate chips and stir until smooth. Stir in remaining one teaspoon of vanilla and remaining ¾ cup of walnuts.
6. Smooth chocolate mixture over pressed dough; crumble remaining dough evenly over surface and press it lightly into filling. Bake 20 minutes. Cool, cut and serve.

Turtle Bars

Makes 24-30 bars

The Ovens' Turtle Bars sandwich pecan-studded caramel filling between a crumbly, buttery cookie crust and a silky chocolate topping. You'll be licking your fingers with these irresistible goodies.

Crust Ingredients:
> 1½ cups flour
> ½ teaspoon baking powder
> ¼ teaspoon salt
> 4 tablespoons cold shortening, in small pieces
> 1 egg
> ¼ teaspoon vanilla

Filling Ingredients:
> ½ pound (2 sticks) butter
> 1 cup brown sugar
> 3 cups chopped pecans
> ¼ cup heavy cream

Glaze Ingredients:
> 6 ounces semisweet chocolate, coarsely chopped
> > OR 1 cup chocolate chips
> 4 tablespoons butter, in small pieces

1. Preheat oven to 350 degrees. Grease a 9-by-13 inch baking pan.
2. *To make crust:* In food processor or by hand, mix flour, baking powder and salt. Cut in shortening until mixture is texture of cornmeal. Mix egg and vanilla, then add to dry mixture. If you are using a food processor, leave machine running while you add egg mixture, but turn it off as soon as egg is poured through. Dough should be crumbly. Spread mixture evenly in pan and press firmly over surface. Bake 5 minutes.
3. *To make filling:* Melt butter and brown sugar. Stir until thoroughly combined. Bring to boil over high heat and cook to soft ball stage (240 degrees on candy thermometer). Remove from heat. Combine pecans and cream and add to caramel mixture. Pour over baked crust and smooth it out. Chill thoroughly.
4. *To make glaze:* Melt chocolate and butter in microwave or over simmering water. Spread evenly over filling. Chill until set and cut into bars.

Sara's Lemon Bars

Makes 24-30 bars

These rich and tart bars are actually better the second day, for the crust will be less crumbly and the filling less sticky after they have refrigerated overnight. Of course, you may not be able to resist eating one or two just after they've cooled out of the oven.

Crust Ingredients:
    1¼ **cups flour**
    ⅓ **cup powdered sugar**
    ¼ **teaspoon salt**
    12 tablespoons cold butter, cut in small pieces

Filling Ingredients:
    5 eggs
    1¼ **cups sugar**
    ⅓ **cup flour**
    Finely grated peel of 1 lemon and 1 orange
    4½ **tablespoons freshly squeezed lemon juice**

For Garnish:
    Powdered sugar

Preheat oven to 350 degrees. To make crust, mix flour, sugar and salt in food processor or blender. Add butter; process until texture of cornmeal. Spread and press into 9-by-13 inch pan; bake 12 minutes. To make filling, beat eggs, sugar and flour until combined. Stir in lemon and orange peel and lemon juice. Pour over baked crust; bake 20 minutes. Cool and refrigerate. Dust with powdered sugar before cutting and serving.

"When from a long-distant past nothing subsists, . . . still, alone, more fragile, but with more vitality, . . . more persistent, more faithful, the smell and taste of things remain poised a long time, like souls, ready to remind us, waiting and hoping for their moment."
—Marcel Proust, *Swann's Way,* 1913

Index

almond(s):
buttermilk scones, Jesse's 101
chicken salad 20
turkey soup 7
Anna's spinach lentil soup 9
antipasto pasta salad 26
appetizers:
artichokes parmesan 3
baked brie 65
scallop sauté 56
scallops, Arienne 4
spinach-stuffed Greek pastries 4
stuffed mushrooms 2
apple(s):
bars, sour cream 118
bread pudding with 88
raisin walnut crêpes 89
walnut blue cheese salad 22
artichokes parmesan 3
avocado filling or dip 81

baked brie 65
Bailey's corn-oat muffins 96
bars:
fudge nut oat brownies 120
lemon, Sara's 122
sour cream apple or cherry 118
turtle 121
bearnaise sauce 47
beef:
carbonnade, Belgian 48
Cornish pasty 50
marinated sirloin or tenderloin strips 48
Ovens meatloaf 46
Ovens of Brittany stir-fry 70
stock xvi
tournedos Henri 46
Belgian beef carbonnade 48
blue cheese:
dressing 31
pasta California 69
salad, apple walnut 22
blueberry muffins 98
bread pudding with apples 88
Brian's chicken tejano 41
brie, baked 65
broccoli:
filling 79
soup, cream of 11
brownies, fudge nut oat 120
butter:
clarified xiii
sweet, unsalted (or margarine?) xii

cadillacs, chocolate 93
Caesar salad 27
cakes: *see pastries*
Cajun shrimp Diane 55
California, pasta 69
carbonnade, Belgian beef 48
carbonara, chicken 38
caramel walnut torte 104

carrot cake with cream cheese frosting 111
celery seed dressing 32
cheese(s):
apple walnut blue cheese salad 22
artichokes parmesan 3
baked brie 65
blue cheese dressing 31
mornay sauce 83
pasta California 69
torte, marble 116
See also specific kinds of cheese
cheesecake, lemon poppyseed 109
cherry bars, sour cream 118
chicken:
almond salad 20
breast preparation xii
carbonara 38
concert chicken salad with pea pods 24
Cordon Bleu 42
Marsala 40
Ovens of Brittany stir-fry 70
pot pie 34
poulet parisienne 36
provençale 39
southwestern turnover 43
stock xvi
tejano, Brian's 41
veronique 42
See also turkey
chili(es):
Mexican-style three bean and three chili soup 10
sauce, Lela Jacobson's 52
chilled cucumber yoghurt soup 18
chocolate:
cadillacs 93
caramel walnut torte 104
chip-coffee muffins 97
farm cakes 113
fudge nut oat brownies 120
marble cheese torte 116
mocha glaze 115
peanut butter chocolate chip cookies 94
pots de creme 108
Queen of Sheba torte 112
triple chip cookies 92
truffle torte 114
turtle bars 121
citron, tarte au 107
clarified butter xiii
classic vinaigrette dressing 23
coffee chocolate chip muffins 97
concert chicken salad with pea pods 24
cookies:
chocolate cadillacs 93
peanut butter 94
peanut butter chocolate chip 94
Prussian tea cakes 95
triple chip 92
Cordon Bleu, chicken 42
Cornish pasty 50
cornmeal whole wheat pancakes 86
Cossack pie 74

cream:
cheese and herb filling 79
cheese frosting 111
of broccoli soup............................... 11
of mushroom soup............................. 12
of vegetable soup 13
types... xiii
creamy garlic dressing...................... 31
crème fraîche xiv
crêpes:
apple raisin walnut 89
French country 80
recipe 73
seafood sauce for pasta and 54
spinach gâteau 72
croutons xiv
cucumber:
dill sauce 60
yoghurt soup 18
curry dressing 30

Danish egg salad 25
desserts: *see pastries, bars and cookies*
Dijon, shrimp 59
dill mustard sauce 64
dips:
avocado...................................... 81
blue cheese 31
chicken/chorizo.............................. 44
curry.. 30
dill mustard.................................. 64
tomato salsa 45
divan sandwich, turkey 65
dough, tart 106

egg(s):
asparagus 90
Benedict 90
discussion.................................... xiv
florentine.................................... 90
hollandaise................................... 82
in herb butter 90
inspirations 90
mornay 83
omelettes 78
Robert 90
salad, Danish 25
salsa.. 45
Santa Fe 90
vegetarian Benedict 90
Virginia's choice.............................. 90
English tea scones 100

farm cakes 113
filling(s):
avocado...................................... 81
broccoli 79
chicken/chorizo.............................. 44
cream cheese and herb 79
French country 80
fish and shellfish:
Cajun shrimp Diane 55
Friday night fish fry 61
gratin of sole 62
poached salmon fillets
  with cucumber dill sauce.................... 60

salmon with dill mustard sauce 60
scallop sauté (with tomato, garlic and parsley).... 56
scallops fettuccine............................ 56
seafood in tomato brandy cream sauce 58
seafood sauce for crêpes or pasta............... 54
shrimp Dijon 59
shrimp with apples and snow peas 57
stock xvi
stuffed trout 62
French country omelette filling 80
Friday night fish fry 61
frostings:
cream cheese................................. 111
mocha glaze 115
fudge nut oat brownies 120

garlic dressing, creamy 31
gâteau, spinach 72
gazpacho 18
gingerbread with honey rum sauce
  Shorewood's 110
glaze, mocha 115
granola, oat bran 89
gratin of sole 62

half-and-half xiii
ham soup, navy bean with 8
heavy cream xiii
Henri, tournedos 46
herb and cream cheese filling 79
hollandaise 82
honey:
rum sauce.................................... 110
squash 68
hot vegetable sandwich 64

Irish potato chowder 14
Italian fried tomatoes 70

Jesse's almond buttermilk scones 101

Lauren's pumpkin bran muffins 99
Lela Jacobson's chili sauce 52
lemon(s):
bars, Sara's.................................. 122
pilaf... 66
poppyseed cheesecake 109
tarte au citron................................ 107
light cream xiii

marble cheese torte 116
marinated:
sirloin or tenderloin strips 48
vegetable salad 29
Marsala, chicken 40
meatloaf, Ovens 46
Mexican-style three bean and three chili soup 10
minestrone 16
mocha glaze 115
mornay sauce 83
muffins:
Bailey's corn-oat 96
blueberry 98
coffee chocolate chip 97
farm cakes 113

Lauren's pumpkin bran 99
oat bran 98
mushroom(s):
  sauce 84
  soup, cream of 12
  stuffed 2
mustard dill sauce 64

navy bean with ham soup 8
New England clam chowder 15

oat bran:
  granola 89
  muffins 98
oatmeal tea cake 102
olive and nut sandwich filling 66
omelette(s):
  recommendations 81
  simple art of making 78
oven-fried or grilled potatoes 67
Ovens:
  meatloaf 46
  of Brittany stir-fry 70

pancakes:
  cornmeal whole wheat 86
  potato 85
  See also crêpes
parisienne, poulet 36
parmesan, discussion of xv
pasta dishes and sauces:
  antipasto pasta salad 26
  Belgian beef carbonnade 48
  chicken carbonara 38
  chicken Marsala 40
  chicken provençale 39
  French country 80
  pasta California 69
  scallop sauté (with tomato, garlic and parsley) 56
  scallops fettuccine 56
  seafood in tomato brandy cream sauce 58
  seafood sauce for crêpes and pasta 54
  vegetarian stroganoff 76
pastries:
  bread pudding with apples 88
  caramel walnut torte 104
  carrot cake with cream cheese frosting 111
  chocolate truffle torte 114
  farm cakes 113
  lemon poppyseed cheesecake 109
  marble cheese torte 116
  oatmeal tea cake 102
  plum cake 117
  pots de creme 108
  Queen of Sheba torte 112
  Shorewood's gingerbread with honey rum sauce .. 110
  spinach-stuffed Greek pastries 4
  tarte au citron 107
  See also bars and cookies
pasty, Cornish 50
peanut butter (and peanut butter
  chocolate chip) cookies 94
pilaf, lemon 66
plum cake 117
poached salmon fillets with cucumber dill sauce ... 60
poppyseed cheesecake, lemon 109

pot pie, chicken 34
potato(es):
  chowder, Irish 14
  oven-fried or grilled 67
  pancakes 85
  rissarole 68
pots de creme 108
poulet parisienne 36
provençale, chicken 39
Prussian tea cakes 95
pudding(s):
  pots de creme 108
  rice 87
  with apples, bread 88
pumpkin bran muffins, Lauren's 99

Queen of Sheba torte 112

raspberry vinaigrette 22
rice:
  lemon pilaf 66
  pudding 87
  salad, wild 21
rissarole potatoes 68
roux xv

salad(s):
  apple walnut blue cheese 22
  antipasto pasta 26
  Caesar 27
  chicken almond 20
  concert chicken with pea pods 24
  Danish egg 25
  marinated vegetable 29
  notions (suggestions) 32
  scallops Arienne 4
  State Street dinner 23
  tropical Waldorf 28
  tuna with walnuts 28
  wild rice 21
salad dressings:
  blue cheese 31
  celery seed 32
  classic vinaigrette 23
  creamy garlic 31
  curry 30
  raspberry vinaigrette 22
salmon:
  fillets with cucumber dill sauce, poached 60
  with dill mustard 60
salsa, tomato 45
sandwiches:
  baked brie 65
  hot vegetable 64
  olive and nut filling for 66
  tuna salad 28
  turkey divan 65
Sara's lemon bars 122
sauce(s):
  bearnaise 47
  carbonara 38
  cucumber dill 60
  dill mustard 64
  for crêpes or pasta, seafood 54
  French country 80
  hollandaise 82

honey rum 110
Lela Jacobson's chili 52
mornay 83
mushroom 84
provençale 39
seafood in tomato brandy cream.............. 58
shrimp with apples and snow peas 57
stir-fry 70
tejano 41
tomato salsa 45
sauté xvi
scallop(s):
   Arienne 4
   fettuccine 56
   sauté (with tomato, garlic and parsley).......... 56
scones:
   English tea 100
   Jesse's almond buttermilk 101
seafood:
   in tomato brandy cream sauce 58
   sauce for crêpes or pasta 54
   stock xvi
   See also "fish and shellfish"
seasoned flour xvi
shrimp:
   Cajun shrimp Diane 55
   Dijon 59
   Ovens of Brittany stir-fry 70
   seafood in tomato brandy cream sauce 58
   with apples and snow peas.............. 57
Shorewood's gingerbread with
   honey rum sauce 110
side dishes:
   baked brie............................. 65
   honey squash.......................... 68
   Italian fried tomatoes 70
   lemon pilaf 66
   oven-fried or grilled potatoes 67
   rissarole potatoes 68
   southern fried tomatoes................. 70
sole, gratin of 62
soup(s):
   cream of broccoli 11
   cream of mushroom 12
   cream of vegetable 13
   cucumber yoghurt, chilled 18
   gazpacho.............................. 18
   Irish potato chowder 14
   Mexican-style three bean and three chili.......... 10
   minestrone 16
   navy bean with ham 8
   New England clam chowder.............. 15
   Spanish country....................... 17
   spinach lentil, Anna's 9
   stock xvi
   turkey almond 7
sour cream apple or cherry bars 118
southern fried tomatoes 70
southwestern turnover...................... 43
Spanish country soup 17
spinach:
   gâteau 72
   lentil soup, Anna's..................... 9
   -stuffed Greek pastries 4
squash, honey 68
State Street dinner salad 23

stir-fry, Ovens of Brittany 70
stock xvi
stroganoff, vegetarian 76
stuffed:
   mushrooms 2
   trout 62

tart dough................................ 106
tarte au citron 107
tea cakes, Prussian 95
tejano, Brian's chicken 41
tenderloin or sirloin strips, marinated 48
tomato(es):
   brandy cream sauce, seafood in 58
   dill soup.............................. 6
   gazpacho.............................. 18
   Italian fried 70
   salsa 45
   scallop sauté, with garlic, parsley and 56
   southern fried 70
tournedos Henri, ... 46
triple chip cookies, ... 92
tropical Waldorf salad, ... 28
trout, stuffed, ... 62
truffle torte, chocolate, ... 114
tuna salad with walnuts, ... 28
turkey:
   almond soup 7
   divan sandwich 65
turnover, southwestern, ... 43
turtle bars, ... 121

vegetable(s):
   Ovens of Brittany stir-fry............... 70
   salad, marinated 29
   sandwich, hot......................... 64
   soup, cream of........................ 13
   stock xvi
vegetarian main courses:
   carbonara sauce (over fettuccine)............ 38
   Cossack pie 74
   omelettes 78
   Ovens of Brittany stir-fry............... 70
   pasta California 69
   provençale sauce (over rice pilaf,
      fettuccine or couscous) 39
   spinach gâteau 72
   vegetarian stroganoff 76
veronique, chicken 42
vinaigrette:
   definition and discussion xvii
   dressing, classic...................... 23
   raspberry 22

Waldorf salad, tropical 28
walnut(s):
   salad, apple walnut blue cheese.............. 22
   torte, caramel 104
   tuna salad with 28
whipping cream xiii
wild rice salad 21